AGAINST THE ODDS

Against the Odds

Black and Minority Ethnic Clinicians and Manchester, 1948 to 2009

Emma L. Jones
Stephanie J. Snow
Foreword by Rajan Madhok

Acknowledgements

Piecing together the beginnings of the history of BME clinicians in Manchester has not been easy. It is a story of individual lives and ambitions against a complex backdrop of post-war labour shortages, the development of the National Health Service (NHS), immigration and emigration, and racial discrimination. We have tried to give recognition to these many factors but recognise that much more work is needed to fully illuminate the complex dynamics.

We are indebted to the many individuals who helped us along the way. Dr Rajan Madhok suggested the project with the aim of stimulating action to address the continuing problems of institutional discrimination within the NHS. We hope that we have gone some way to addressing his concerns and we are especially grateful for his commitment to learning from the past. Responsibility for the text and arguments however rests solely with the authors.

The work has been carried out in the Wellcome Unit of the Centre for the History of Science, Technology and Medicine (CHSTM) at the University of Manchester, and we are grateful to the Director of the Centre, Professor Michael Worboys, for his support. Professor John Pickstone has been involved with the project from its beginnings, helping to shape its final form and encouraging us along the way. Colleagues within CHSTM have provided support and bonhomie; Stephanie is also grateful to her colleagues at the National Primary Care Research and Development Centre at the University of Manchester where she is currently on secondment.

The majority of our primary evidence was obtained from interviews and we thank all those whose biographies appear in the following pages for their time and willingness to reflect on often difficult memories. Without them this work would not have been possible.

For their help in providing access to other relevant material was nothing compared to the 'polite violence' he experienced in Southern England. Some form of discrimination in society is therefore inevitable. I also know that it is not easy to address such fundamental aspects of human nature. This should not however deter us from aspiring to a fairer NHS where merit rather than heritage decides your future. We must try and get things right for the future generations of clinicians in the NHS. With increasing numbers of BME and women students in medicine, the white male student is in danger of becoming the new minority. If we do not create meritocracy as the organising principle for the NHS we will end up with further polarisation.

I very much hope that this review will help us all – the fair minded majority – to explore how we can create a win-win for BME (and all) clinicians and the NHS. Having 'dun roaming' Manchester is home now. Mancunians love a challenge and I hope that we can lead the way in making the NHS a fairer place. There is a lot to gain and nothing to lose.

With very best wishes
Rajan Madhok
Medical Director, NHS Manchester

Introduction

In Britain, around 30% of nurses and doctors are from black and minority ethnic (BME) groups.[1] The proportion of BME clinicians working in British health services rose enormously between the creation of the National Health Service (NHS) in 1948 and the 1980s and has stabilised over the last twenty years or so. However, it is well-documented that throughout this period, BME clinicians have been and continue to be over-represented in the lower grades of the professions, under-represented in senior managerial positions, and work in the less popular areas; fewer than 10% of NHS senior managers and only 1% of NHS chief executives have a minority ethnic background. Discrimination, it seems, continues to hinder equality of opportunity and experience.

This book examines the history of BME nurses and doctors in and around Manchester since the Second World War.[2] Since 1948, significant proportions of the NHS workforce in the city have been made up of nurses, midwives, health visitors and doctors from minority ethnic groups, most of whom have been recruited from overseas. Yet very little is publicly known about the experiences of these individuals and the particular challenges they have faced in their chosen careers. Here we aim to address this knowledge gap.

In conducting this study we talked to BME nurses and doctors who have worked in the Manchester area over the last sixty or so years. By so doing we contribute to the growing body of literature that seeks to recover the voices of those who are seldom heard in traditional social and political histories of the NHS. An entire cohort of workers who entered the NHS in its formative years is fast approaching retirement; our capturing of their stories now will ensure that they enter the collective memory. In some respects, our work builds on the North West Strategic Health Authority's *Celebrating Our Diversity and Multi-Ethnic Contribution* exhibition for the Sixtieth Anniversary of the NHS in 2008 which highlighted the personal experiences, achievements, and challenges of thirty-four BME health service workers in the area.[3]

Primarily, this book is directed at professional leaders and policy-makers in Manchester; but there is nothing to suggest that Manchester's experiences are unique. We hope that the book will be of interest to all those dealing with racial equality in all NHS settings. The current predicted shortfalls in certain fields of nursing and medicine, and the recent expansion in the recruitment of overseas-qualified clinicians, echo the dynamics that shaped the first sixty years of the NHS, locally and nationally. Knowing what happened in the past might help us to better understand current trends, and to avoid the same mistakes in the decades to come.

Our Sources

One of the strengths of this study is that we have approached BME clinicians as a collective group. This has allowed us to identify the many similarities in experiences between BME doctors and nurses with regard to migrating to Britain; struggling with professional training and career progression; working in unpopular specialties and deprived areas; and experiencing institutional discrimination in NHS organisations and social discrimination by patients and colleagues. It has also illuminated the considerable differences between the two BME groups: the majority of nurses came to Britain from the African Caribbean whereas the majority of doctors originated from South Asia; nurses often remain in a locality due to family commitments, whereas doctors' mobility tends to be dictated by job opportunities; and although there are indications that doctors have overcome some of the barriers of discrimination, the evidence shows that nurses continue to experience difficulties. We suggest that many of the differences between the two groups can be better understood by mapping the history of BME clinicians onto the wider histories of nursing and medicine. Discrimination has a long history and we can best understand it, not just as a one-dimensional problem centred on the mass employment of overseas workers in the NHS during the last half of the twentieth century, but rather as a multi-dimensional problem that has much to do with the long-term structures and cultures of the professions of nursing and medicine.

Owing to time-constraints and difficulties in locating individuals who had spent sufficient time working in the Manchester area and were willing to be interviewed, our sample is, regrettably, small. Nor is it representative either in terms of BME groups or gender.

A total of three nurses, one midwife, two health visitors, and eight doctors were interviewed. Of the nurses, midwives and health visitors, five were of West Indian origin (one British born), and one of African origin. All had trained in Britain, and all were female. Only one of the nurses we interviewed did her initial nurse training in the Manchester area, but all eventually came to work in the city. At the time of interview, two respondents had moved out of nursing: one into academic nursing/health policy research and development and another into social work. Of the eight doctors, seven were of Asian origin (one British born), and one of Turkish origin. Of these, six doctors were overseas-trained, and two doctors (one Asian born, one British born) were trained in Britain. We spoke to only one female doctor who was of Turkish origin. Those we interviewed were currently employed in hospital medicine, general practice, public health, academic research and the voluntary sector. Some left one field of employment for another; others combined more than one. Detailed career biographies can be found at the end of chapters 4 and 5. The interviews were informal and unstructured, but a number of common themes were explored including family background, education, migration to Britain, experiences of recruitment, training, employment and promotion, problems encountered, and their feelings about their experiences.

It is also necessary to acknowledge that the configuration of the interview itself may have impacted on what *was* said and what was *not* said. Those asked to talk about their working-lives and contribution to the NHS on tape to a complete stranger may understandably choose to present their stories in a positive light, but we risked asking our interviewees to recall what might well have been painful experiences. Indeed, for some of our interviewees it was possibly the first time they had been asked to recall particular episodes, and had spoken of them out loud. Generally interviewees appeared open and frank in discussing their experiences, but there were occasions when we sensed that some became more reserved in their responses, particularly when referring to specific incidents of discrimination involving senior staff that may be identifiable. For a number of our interviewees this was also not the first time that their life stories had been recorded; in such cases there was the danger that the resulting account constituted a well-rehearsed, official narrative.

Many of those we interviewed did not generally speak of their experiences in terms of racism although all of them expressed awareness and experience of difference in their personal and working lives. This is not an unusual finding. Research has shown that racism – discrimination against individuals on the basis of race or ethnicity – is a complex phenomenon. It can be subtle or overt and can occur on a personal and an institutional level where it is also 'mediated by complexities of organisational control, power and social relations'.[4] The historian Joanna Bornat has written of the common pattern amongst medical migrants of presenting their life stories as one of ambition through hard work and successful achievement. Within such a narrative, other peoples' behaviour is either explained in terms of generalised prejudice and ignorance (for example, racist comments made by patients and their relatives), or as obstacles that were overcome in the pursuit of career development (as with the behaviour of colleagues, senior staff or institutional practices, especially in the areas of recruitment and promotion).[5]

In view of the small numbers, we believe that the interviews can best stand as illustrative cases of the key concerns that have affected many BME clinicians over the period. We would stress however that the experiences of these particular individuals may not necessarily be the norm. Potential interviewees were identified largely by word-of-mouth. Inevitably, many of the individuals we spoke to have had markedly successful careers, and are well known in their respective fields. Their case histories are, on the whole, stories of achievement, albeit against the odds. For this reason we draw on the wider histories of immigration and racial discrimination and where possible use statistics to provide a backdrop to these individual stories although data on BME health workers has only begun to be collected recently. In 1995, ethnic monitoring became mandatory in the hospital sector and in 2000, the NHS became subject to the Race Relations Act which placed a duty on all Trusts to monitor the numbers of staff in post, applicants for employment, training, and promotion by reference to ethnicity. Statistical comparison can be tricky however as the processes of classification, manipulation and presentation of data differ between Trusts.

Structure

The remainder of the book is split into five chapters. Chapters 2 and 3 set the scene, exploring the historical connections between the NHS, shortages of nurses and doctors, and labour migration, first nationally and then locally. We also explore attitudes to mass migration in post-war Britain and Manchester, providing the broader context against which attitudes to overseas nurses and doctors must be read. Chapters 4 and 5 feature our case histories, drawing on our interviews with the nurses and doctors who have supported the development of the NHS in and around Manchester for over sixty years. We explore how these particular BME clinicians have fared in the NHS, comparing their individual experiences to those of others at the time, as well as to more recent cohorts. Finally, in Chapter 6 we summarise our findings and suggest ways in which they might be used to benefit the BME clinicians of the future.

2

Post-War Britain: Labour and Immigration

The creation of a national health service at the end of the Second World War was part of a radical programme of reforms introduced by Clement Attlee's newly elected Labour government. Alongside the nationalisation of private industries and utilities, a major home-building programme, and the promise of full employment, Labour planned to create a comprehensive, universal system of health care in Britain, free at the point of delivery, from 'cradle to grave' and designed to 'secure improvement in the physical and mental health of the people'.[1]

The NHS which came into operation on 5 July 1948 brought together hospitals, primary care, and public health in a tripartite structure that represented a political compromise between the government and the different interest groups. Municipal and voluntary hospitals were nationalised; GPs, dentists, opticians and community pharmacists joined the service as independent contractors; and public health remained with local authorities.[2] On the appointed day the government took charge of 2,688 hospitals providing some 480,000 beds (190,000 of which were in hospitals for the mentally ill).[3] Control of the country's voluntary hospitals was exercised through local and regional boards on which doctors, philanthropists and councillors would be represented. The more prestigious teaching hospitals reported directly to the Ministry of Health, and their elite doctors, or 'consultants', got paid special financial awards for giving up some of their private work for hospital work. Free care from GPs extended the benefits of Lloyd George's insurance scheme, created in 1911 to provide care for working men, to all patients. The NHS proved immensely successful with the public and its popularity was reflected in a large rise in patient numbers. The number of inpatients rose from 2.9 million in 1949 to 3.5 million by 1953. Outpatient numbers rose from 6.1 million to

6.7 million and during the same period, millions of people signed on with a GP, and there was huge demand for dentures, spectacles and hearing aids.[4]

While planners had anticipated that costs of the NHS might fall once the backlog of untreated illness had been dealt with, in fact the take-up of free medical and dental care caused costs to rise dramatically.[5] Within months of its launch, Aneurin Bevan, the Minister for Health, warned colleagues that the costs of the new system were almost 30% higher than originally estimated. With the economy weakened by war, and resources needed for the building of new homes, the construction of new hospitals became a distant prospect.[6]

Over the first decade of the NHS, the spread of specialists and expanding technologies was underpinned by unprecedented increases in the medical and nursing workforce. Between 1949 and 1958 the medical workforce increased by 30% in England and 50% in Scotland; the nursing and midwifery workforce increased by 26% across Britain.[7] Unsurprisingly, many parts of the NHS struggled to recruit enough staff to sustain this expansion.

NHS Labour Shortages

The problems of staffing the new health service were exacerbated by a national post-war labour shortage. After 1945, a large proportion of Britain's male population were retained in the Armed Forces, while many civilians retired from waged labour on account of their age.[8] Many of the women who had entered industries where little or no female labour had been employed prior to the war either left their jobs voluntarily or were forced out of them; many were finding employment in sectors that had now opened up to them, such as secretarial work, teaching, and the civil service.[9] The raising of the school leaving age to fifteen and emigration were also factors that intensified labour shortages, particularly in low-paid jobs that British people were no longer willing to do.[10] The health services were no exception; the NHS experienced a severe shortage of nurses, midwives, ancillary workers, cleaners, cooks and porters.

Staffing crises in British hospitals had been identified long before the establishment of the NHS. Concern over the shortage of nurses had been the subject of numerous government inquiries since the 1930s, which blamed low recruitment on inadequate training, poor pay, and the marriage bar.[11] During the war, hospital domestic and nursing work had been regarded as vital to the war effort and had attracted a large number of women into national service. After the war, hospitals were forced to compete for female labour alongside other sectors of the economy and concerns over the shortage of nursing and domestic staff resurfaced. The most severe shortages were in hospitals for the chronically sick, in mental hospitals and in geriatric nursing, all of them unpopular areas of nursing. Additionally, workers from the Irish Republic had provided a major 'internal' reserve of labour for low-paid nursing and ancillary hospital jobs prior to 1939.[12] A downturn in Irish migration after 1945, and a formalisation of the previously free-flowing recruitment procedures between England and the Irish Free State, contributed to the problem of filling vacancies in the new health service.[13]

By the end of 1945, shortages had reached such levels that doubts were raised over whether the service would be able to cope if a high incidence of epidemic disease should occur that winter.[14] A government report, *Staffing the Hospitals: An Urgent National Need*, published in December 1945, identified the need for around 30,000 nurses and midwives and 12,000 domestic and other health service workers. In 1947, a report by the Ministry of Health Working Party on the Recruitment and Training of Nurses reported an immediate shortage of between 9,000 and 10,000 trained nurses and midwives. It also estimated that the current force of 88,000 trained nurses would need to increase by a minimum of between 120,000 to 125,000, with some 14,000 nursing orderlies alongside, if they were to provide properly for the requirements of the proposed NHS, to improve standards of nurse training, and to combat wastage during training.[15] The report recommended the recruitment of more male nurses, the lifting of restrictions on married nurses staying in post, the introduction of part-time employment, and the awarding of full student status to all nurse students, so as to relieve them of the less attractive domestic work.[16] Recruitment campaigns encouraged women and the retired to enter, re-enter, or remain in employment, and employers to operate more flexible working conditions such as part-time working. By 1948, however, the number of nursing vacancies in the NHS stood at 54,000, with shortages particularly acute in sanatoria and mental nursing where staff turnover was high, and the geographical isolation of the institutions made it difficult to recruit locally.[17]

Recruitment of Overseas Nursing Staff

With general recruitment campaigns in Britain failing to solve the problem of nursing and nursing orderly shortages, institutions began recruiting from continental Europe.[18] Beginning in 1946, the British government had resorted to a variety of migrant labour schemes to deal with unskilled worker shortages in a range of essential industries including agriculture, coal mining, and the textile industries, as well as hospital domestic employment. These schemes began with the recruitment of Prisoners of War (POWs) and exiled Poles who were already in the country and were given the option to work and settle in Britain rather than be repatriated. Next came workers from countries such as France and Belgium, recruited under contract to do specific jobs for a specified amount of time. Displaced Persons living in refugee camps in the British occupied zones of Austria and West Germany became the third source of cheap foreign labour for the British government.

Under European migrant labour schemes the number of trainee nurses recruited from countries such as France, Italy, Spain, Portugal, and Germany working in Britain grew from 584 in 1947 to 1,050 by 1950.[19] The recruitment of Displaced Persons began with the drafting of one thousand Baltic women (originating from Latvia, Lithuania, and Estonia) into Britain to take up residential domestic work in TB sanatoria in October 1946. It was known as the 'Baltic Cygnet Scheme'. A few months later, the scheme was extended to include a further five thousand women for domestic work in general hospitals.[20] This was known as 'Westward Ho!' By 1953, some 3,891 Baltic women from the British zone had been recruited for domestic work in hospitals and institutions.[21] Despite these efforts, staffing shortfalls remained. Not all recruitment was coordinated nationally; it was often done by individual hospitals, either through advertisements or recruiting visits to Europe.[22] Language difficulties led to poor retention rates,[23] and Western European countries also had their own labour shortages to contend with. In 1947, for example, the Ministry of Health unsuccessfully approached four Scandinavian governments in a bid to recruit midwives but all reported similar labour shortages.[24]

Unable to secure sufficient numbers of European workers, the British government began to look further afield to its colonies and former colonies in the West Indies, including Jamaica, Barbados, Trinidad, the Windward Isles, and St Kitts. The birth of the NHS in 1948 coincided with the arrival in Britain of the first ships from the Caribbean, *The Empire Windrush* and the *SS Orbita*, bringing with them several hundred migrant workers. Between the end of the war and 1958, some 125,000 West Indians arrived in Britain, escaping high unemployment, low wages, and lack of opportunity in their home countries.[25] Jamaica had a long tradition of labour migration, frequently to the US, but new US restrictions on migrants in 1952 meant that many West Indians turned to Britain instead. By the end of 1958 some 55,000 Indians and Pakistanis had also arrived, many having lost land, homes, and jobs following the separation of India and Pakistan after Independence.[26] The Nationality Act 1948, which granted full citizenship to those from the Commonwealth, aided the emigration of West Indians and Asians, allowing them to enter Britain freely, to work and to settle with their families.

These migrants were overwhelmingly stereotyped as unskilled manual workers. For the government and employers, they were a means of filling the jobs which indigenous workers were unwilling to do, so that while 27% of the women and 46% of the men who settled in Britain from the West Indies in this period were actually skilled manual workers, many newcomers found themselves accepting a job of lower status than they would have had in their home country.[27] Some West Indians were actively recruited in their home countries by British businesses and industries experiencing acute labour shortages. These included London Transport (which recruited Barbadians in the 1950s, and Jamaicans and Trinidadians in the 1960s), the British hotel and restaurant industry (which recruited from Barbados), and the NHS (from across the West Indies).[28]

As early as 1949 the Ministries of Health and Labour, in conjunction with the Colonial Office, the General Nursing Council and the Royal College of Nursing launched campaigns to recruit hospital staff directly from the Caribbean. Recruitment was aimed at three main categories of worker: hospital auxiliary staff, including orderlies, receptionists, cooks, pantry workers and telephonists; nurses or trainee nurses; and domestic workers, such as laundry workers.[29] Senior NHS staff from Britain travelled to the Caribbean to recruit, and vacancies were often published in local papers. In 1949, for example, the *Barbados Beacon* advertised for nursing auxiliaries to work in hospitals across Britain, including those in Manchester.[30] Applicants were to be aged between 18 and 30, literate, and willing to commit to a three-year contract.[31] By 1955 there were official nursing recruitment programmes across 16 British colonies and former colonies.

Over the next two decades, the British colonies and former colonies provided a constant supply of cheap labour to meet staffing shortages in the NHS, and the number of West Indian women entering Britain to work in the NHS grew steadily until the early 1970s. By the end of 1965, there were 3,000–5,000 Jamaican nurses working in British hospitals, many of them concentrated in London and the Midlands.[32] It has been estimated that by 1972, 10,566 students had been recruited from abroad, and that by 1977 overseas recruits represented 12% of the student nurse and midwife population in Britain, of which 66% came from the Caribbean.[33]

Recruitment of Overseas Doctors

No sooner had the recruitment of nurses been tackled than the NHS faced a shortage of doctors. When the NHS was created all medical staff were reviewed and graded. In many smaller hospitals doctors were classed as 'Senior Hospital Medical Officers' rather than Consultants, while others left the hospital service to become GPs. In the prominent teaching hospitals, most clinicians were given consultant status. They were now paid for their hospital work, but were also free to do some private practice. A few top consultants were also bestowed 'merit awards' as compensation for any loss of income from their private practice resulting from their hospital commitments.

The hospital service, though led by consultants, was dependent upon a large army of junior doctors (and nurses) to support and deliver patient care. The creation of supernumerary posts for young doctors returning from the war to train as consultants went some way to meeting the demand for manpower on the wards, but supernumeraries tended to be absorbed into the middle and senior levels of staffing. In 1944, the Goodenough Committee had recommended expanding medical schools to relieve the shortage of doctors. The 1957 Willink Committee investigated the number of doctors required by the NHS and decided that student numbers should be cut because there was a risk of overproduction. Taking into account the minimum five-year period of training, the Committee concluded that reducing medical student intake by 10% between 1961 and 1975 would keep numbers in balance. Even before the Committee's recommendations were made public some medical schools had begun to reduce their student intakes because they had been swamped by demobbed-servicemen taking medicine, as well as the normal intake of school leavers.[34] Within months of the report's publication, it became evident that a shortage of medical personnel was imminent.[35]

In retrospect it is clear that the Willink Committee's estimates failed to anticipate the need for extra doctors to improve future health service and to meet the requirements of a growing population. These underestimates drove the first mass-wave of medical recruitment from India, Pakistan, Bangladesh and Sri Lanka and by 1960, between 30 and 40% of all junior doctors in the NHS were from these countries.[36] The emigration of thousands of doctors from the Indian Sub-continent to work in the NHS during the 1960s and 1970s built on Britain's historical links with its ex-colonial territories, especially India. As a direct result of colonial rule, by the time of Indian Independence in 1947 Indian medical schools and hospital administration ran along the lines of the British model. Medical education and training were delivered in English, and geared towards meeting the requirements of the General Medical Council. This ensured that Indian-trained doctors would be able to work in Britain, and it encouraged overseas medical graduates to come to Britain to gain further training and experience that they would then take home.[37] Hence, long before the first significant wave of medical migration in the 1960s, Asian doctors had a presence in Britain.[38] One estimate suggests that by 1945 there were already 1,000 Asian doctors working in Britain, some 200 of them in London alone.[39] By the 1950s, their number had risen to 3,000.[40] The important contribution of these overseas doctors to the early years of the NHS was openly acknowledged. In 1961, Lord Cohen of Birkenhead told the House of Lords: 'The Health Service would have collapsed if it had not been for the enormous influx from junior doctors from such countries as India and Pakistan'.[41]

In 1963 the Conservative Health Minister, Enoch Powell, who would later lead the call for stricter controls on immigration, launched a campaign to recruit trained doctors from overseas to fill the manpower shortages caused by NHS expansion. Some 18,000 of them were recruited from India and Pakistan. Powell praised these doctors, who he said, 'provide a useful and substantial reinforcement of the staffing of our hospitals and who are an advertisement to the world of British medicine and British hospitals.'[42] Many of those recruited had several years of experience in their home countries and arrived to gain further medical experience, training, or qualification. In 1968, the recruitment of overseas doctors was fuelled again by the predictions of further medical shortages by the Todd Committee which recommended expanding medical schools. By 1971, 31% of all doctors working in the NHS in England were born and qualified overseas.[43] Whilst thousands of overseas doctors entered Britain during this period, large numbers of UK-trained doctors left the country to work abroad.

In addition to underestimating the numbers of doctors required by the expanding NHS, the Willink Committee had notably failed to take account of the significant numbers of British-trained white doctors who were leaving the country to work abroad, mainly in the United States and Canada, because of the poor pay and conditions of the NHS.[44] Between 1954 and 1963, an estimated 3,425 doctors from Great Britain emigrated permanently to Australia, New Zealand, Canada, the United States, South Africa, and Southern Rhodesia (now Zimbabwe) alone.[45] By the late 1960s, Henry Miller, Professor of Neurology at Newcastle

Figure 2.1   Number of doctors emigrating from England, Scotland and Wales, 1948–1963

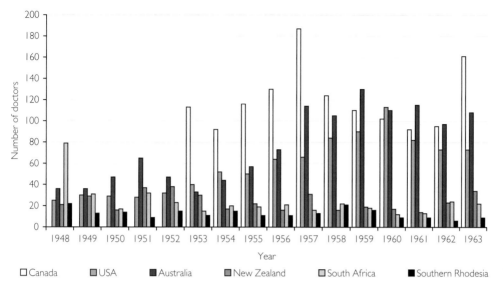

Source: J. Seale, 'Medical Emigration from Great Britain and Ireland', British Medical Journal, 1 (1964), 1173–1178.

University and chairman of the British Medical Association's Committee for Planning, estimated that the annual emigration of British-trained doctors amounted to between 30 and 50% of the annual number of medical graduates.[46]

Attitudes towards Post-War Migrants

Immigration to Britain had been occurring for thousands of years. Trade and mercantile interests brought some of the first settlers to Britain in the medieval and early-modern periods, among them Jewish businessmen and tradesmen, German merchants, and Italian bankers. Others arrived as refugees, fleeing famine or persecution, including the Huguenots (French Protestants) fleeing Catholic France during the sixteenth, seventeenth and eighteenth centuries; Irish people from the 1790s and particularly in the wake of the Great Famine in the 1840s; and Jews at the end of the nineteenth century, as a result of pogroms in western Russia and eastern Poland. Trade within the ever-expanding British Empire also ensured that new flows of people included sailors and seamen from South East Asia and India (known as Lascars), China, and West Africa, many of whom settled and formed communities in the port cities of Liverpool and London. Meanwhile, the demands of the industrial revolution provided work for Irish labourers, and also continued to attract merchants and manufacturers from Europe. Other Europeans arrived throughout the nineteenth century, including Germans and Italians. In the twentieth century, British universities also attracted a significant number of students from overseas countries, including Africa, India, Europe and America. While most students returned home, some chose to settle permanently after qualifying.[47]

From the early twentieth century onwards the British government began to exert control over the entry, employment, and deportation of people who were not deemed to be British subjects. The 1905 Aliens Act refused entry to those deemed 'undesirable' – the diseased, the insane, criminals, and those likely to be a burden on public funds. The legislation was an anti-Semitic response to the inflow of Jews from Russia and Eastern Europe who were fleeing persecution and poverty, but it was also used against other communities of migrants who had recently established themselves, including the Chinese. Jewish immigrants, in particular, were blamed for the complex economic and social problems experienced in the areas where they settled, predominantly the East End of London, and fears were expressed that their presence was creating competition for jobs, housing, and amenities. In 1920, a new Aliens Order established procedures by which 'aliens' seeking employment in Britain were issued with work permits. In the post-war period, it was this legislation that facilitated the recruitment of aliens to work in Britain after 1945, for specified periods of time, and for specified employers, although some flexibility was introduced. As contracted, and thereby controlled sources of labour, both Displaced Persons and those Europeans recruited through migrant labour schemes were severely limited in terms of their economic, social, and political rights.

Medical immigration was part of the mass migration to Britain from 1945 onwards which was to change the nation's ethnic landscape in an unprecedented way and bring racial tensions to a new pitch. Before the war, only 5% of the population had been born outside Britain and these individuals were mainly from families with English and Scottish origins, born whilst their parents were abroad.[48] Earlier immigrant communities like the Irish and the Jews had suffered from discrimination and often struggled to gain housing and employment. That immigrants drained vital resources from host communities proved an enduring element of anti-immigration rhetoric, as indeed did the popular myth that all migrants were unskilled. Prejudice against black and Asian people arriving in the first wave of mass migration was swiftly manifested. The employment of black and Asian workers was resisted by white trade unionists who insisted on imposing a quota system on the numbers of overseas workers that were employed. Within the NHS, concern that the importing of migrant workers was likely to create tensions of a more personal nature was recognised in a 1949 Home Office memo that stated: 'it has been found that the susceptibilities of patients tended to set an upper limit on the proportion of coloured workers who could be employed either as nurses or domiciliaries'.[49] Migrants endured verbal and physical abuse both within and outside the workplace.

From the late 1950s onwards, populist antagonism towards immigrants, specifically from the Commonwealth countries, increased. A series of 'race riots' in Nottingham and London in 1958 brought the discontents of immigration to the fore, although they were mostly white-led disturbances stirred up by sensational journalism.[50] Reports of public fears that migrant workers were taking away jobs, houses, and hospital beds from white British citizens were common. In reality, most migrants found it harder than the host population to find suitable housing and employment, and as later stories will testify, workers arriving in Britain during this period from the West Indies and later from South Asia were widely discriminated against in the workplace. Their children, many of whom were born in Britain, grew up in the shadow of aggression and harassment. West Indian children, for example, were particularly disadvantaged in the education system. In the 1950s and 1960s, for example, a disproportionate number of West Indian migrant children were classified as 'educationally subnormal' and placed in special schools and units. Until the 1960s, the state school system also made no special provision for South Asian migrant children, many of whom arrived knowing very little English.[51]

Hostility and prejudice towards post-war migrants in Britain was not only registered through popular protest. As Peter Fryer argues, 'racism' after 1945 'was institutionalised, legitimized and nationalized'.[52] With virtually every new wave of migration after 1945, measures to reduce the flow of immigrants were taken by the government. The 1948 Nationality Act, which had granted British citizenship to citizens of British colonies and former British colonies, was under attack by the 1960s. In 1962, the then Conservative Government introduced the Commonwealth Immigrants Bill, restricting the admission of Commonwealth settlers to those who had been issued with employment vouchers. In the eighteen-month period before the Act was passed, many new arrivals came to Britain. This large influx stoked popular fears of uncontrolled immigration, which sustained calls for increased controls.

In 1968, a new Labour Government introduced a second Commonwealth Immigrants Act, which distinguished between

British passport holders, with the right to live in the Britain, and those without. Those with the right to live in Britain were defined as patrials, i.e. persons entitled to citizenship either through birth, adoption, naturalisation, or with a British-born grandparent, or as a citizen of Britain and its former colonies who had settled and resided in Britain for five years.[53] The law was rushed through with the primary purpose of restricting the entry into Britain of Kenyan Asians, driven out by the 'Africanisation' policies of the Kenyan government. As British passport holders, Kenyan Asians had had, up to this point, unconditional rights of entry. While this new piece of legislation applied to all Commonwealth countries, including Australia, New Zealand, and Canada, it was more unlikely that people from the New Commonwealth would qualify as patrials, thereby creating a division between white and black Commonwealth citizens.

The passage of the Commonwealth Immigrants Bill proved divisive. On the one hand it was attacked as a racist and shameful piece of legislation, and the government were accused of surrendering to racist hysteria. On the other hand, it was praised for being in touch with the opinions of the working and lower-middle class electorate.[54] Shortly after the Bill was passed, Enoch Powell made his now infamous "Rivers of Blood Speech" in which he attacked black and Asian immigration. Increasingly stringent immigration controls were accompanied by attempts to improve race relations. The first Race Relations Acts were passed in 1965 and 1968, but though these outlawed incitement to racial hatred they did nothing to address discrimination taking place in areas such as housing and employment. Labour also established both the National Committee for Commonwealth Immigrants and the Race Relations Board, statutory bodies which were set up to promote integration, liaison and conciliation, and to ensure compliance with the Race Relations Act. Implicit in many of these measures too was the notion that the 'race' problem lay with the immigrants themselves. Indeed, behind all attempts to stem the inflow of black and Asian people into Britain after 1945 was the assumption that their presence rather than white racism was the root cause of social unrest.

In 1971, a returning Conservative government introduced the Immigration Act, ending primary migration from the Commonwealth. Non-patrials were now only allowed to enter Britain for employment if they had a work permit for a particular job for a limited period of time. As work permits carried no right to settlement, hereafter, those New Commonwealth migrants entering Britain effectively became contract labour.[55] (An exception was made for the 30,000 or so Ugandan Asians, holding British passports, who were expelled from the country by Idi Amin in 1972). The 1981 British Nationality Act established under Margaret Thatcher's government, introduced three tiers of citizenship: British Citizens, who had the right to abode in Britain; and Citizens of Dependent Territories and British Overseas Citizens, who had no such right to do so. The act also removed the automatic right to citizenship of those born in Britain, except to parents who were settled in the Britain and not subject to immigration controls.[56] Subsequent immigration controls in the 1980s, including the introduction of visas and the withdrawal of the unconditional right to family reunion, further reduced the rights of Commonwealth citizens.

As we have noted, the flow into Britain of economic labour migrants and refugees displaced by conflict, persecution, and the break up of old empires has been continuous since 1945. Most recently it has been refugees from the former Yugoslavia and Romania, and from Afghanistan, West Africa, and Zimbabwe who have sought asylum and a better future in Britain. In 2007, the non-British born population in Britain was an estimated 6.3 million people (10.6% of the total British population). The five most common non-British countries of birth in Britain were India, the Republic of Ireland, Poland, Pakistan, and Germany.[57] According to the last census in 2001, 92% of the British population were white, which included a significant number of non-English white minorities, such as those from Ireland and the rest of the EU. A further 4% of the population were Asian or Asian-British, 2% were black or black-British, and 1.5% were of mixed origin.[58]

Immigration Controls and Overseas Clinicians

In parallel with restricting immigration, successive British governments looked to the Commonwealth to solve labour shortages in key sectors of the economy, particularly education and the health service. Exceptions to immigration controls were made for essential and well-qualified staff, and hence both nurses and doctors were exempt from the immigration controls imposed in the 1960s. In general, the men and women who came to work in the NHS were welcomed throughout this period of political agitation. Their professional status distinguished them from the mass of migrants, most of whom were classified as unskilled.

In spite of his later vocal opposition to black and Asian immigration in general, Health Minister Enoch Powell championed the recruitment of overseas nurses in the early 1960s. As historian Charles Webster suggests, this apparent anomaly was perhaps

Figure 2.2. Overseas-born population as a percentage of total UK population

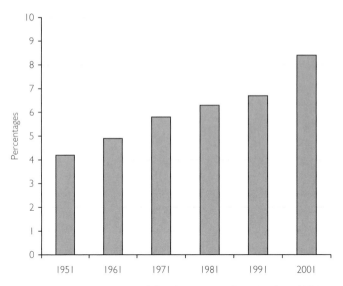

Source: International Migration, Office for National Statistics, June 2004.

because the immigration of nurses not only 'provided a plentiful supply of cheap labour, reduced wastage, and undermined the shortage argument' but also 'strengthened his hand in pressing for a strong line against the nurses' pay claim, which itself was his chief weapon in his wider campaign to induce colleagues to adopt a more aggressive approach to the control of public sector pay.'[59] Immigrant nurses were therefore an expedient means of providing political leverage.

The situation altered by the 1970s. Immigration laws undermined the employment rights of overseas nurses. The automatic right of entry to prospective nurses from the Commonwealth was withdrawn with the passing of the 1971 Immigration Act. In 1983, work permits for nurses were also abolished prohibiting further entry of overseas nurses to train in Britain. A report for the Commission of Racial Equality, published in 1983, found a higher proportion of trained overseas–born nurses, than overseas-born nurses in training. It also stated that less than 9% of nurses employed by the NHS were born in developing countries.[60]

In the 1970s, overseas nurses also came under increasing scrutiny from the professional nursing body. In its evidence to the Briggs Committee on nursing in Britain in 1971, the Royal College of Nursing (RCN) specifically identified overseas nurses as a distinct problem in nursing manpower shortages.[61] With little evidence to support their claims, the RCN not only stated that the educational ability of overseas nurses accepted for training was often sub-standard, but also blamed falling recruitment and retention of trained staff on an 'undue reliance on overseas recruitment.'[62] The argument being that if working conditions and wages were improved enough student nurses from Britain could be recruited and there would be no need to depend on overseas labour.

By the late 1980s the NHS was again facing serious problems in the retention and recruitment of nursing staff, much as it had done in 1948. The problem now involved chronic shortages of both trainees and qualified nurses. Nursing's popularity as a career choice among school leavers had declined markedly. Changing social expectations and financial constraints meant that young people were now seeking better-paid job opportunities in other sectors of the economy.[63] Meanwhile, an estimated 30,000 nurses were leaving the NHS every year; their departure blamed on long-standing problems associated with low salary levels and the pressures of the job. Unable to rely on a steady flow of overseas trainees and qualified nurses the government and health authorities launched national and local recruitment campaigns, which had some success in reaching their target group of school leavers.[64]

The crisis in nursing manpower has continued. By 1998, there were reports that the shortages in newly qualified nurses were approximating 8,000 a year.[65] The new NHS plan introduced by Tony Blair's New Labour government in the late 1990s led to a planned and funded expansion of the NHS. It also created a need to rapidly increase the numbers of nurses and doctors working within the health service. While the number of British training places was increased, this did not solve the immediate demand for workforce growth and so between 1998 and 2005 international recruitment once again became one of the government's key strategies in tackling the chronic shortage of qualified nurses in the NHS.

Under political pressure to adopt an ethical approach to international recruitment, particularly from African countries, the government issued a directive in 1999 banning all NHS trusts from recruiting from the developing world, except from named countries where there was known to be a surplus, including the Philippines, India, and China. Some developing countries with a surplus of nurses sought to maximise the benefits of this opportunity; the government of the Philippines established a development plan which encouraged nurses to train abroad and send some of their earnings home.[66] In 2002–2003 more than half of the nurses newly registered with the Nursing and Midwifery Council had trained outside Britain.[67] As in earlier periods, the geographical distribution of these nurses was differentiated across the country with higher proportions of foreign-trained nurses working in large cities like Manchester, Birmingham, and Bristol. The new ethical Code of Practice (which was formalised in 2004) did not prevent individuals from developing countries applying for jobs or travelling to Britain for training. Nor did the directive extend to nurses recruited by commercial recruitment agencies or private sector employers. Hence, many international nurses from 'no-go' areas of recruitment, particularly in Africa, continued to find their way to working in the NHS via independent care homes and hospitals.

Recent figures show a reduction in the numbers of overseas nurses, midwives and health visitors registering to work in Britain.[68] Since September 2006, overseas nurses have been required to complete a twenty-day Overseas Nurses Programme (ONP), providing a period of supervised practice placement and adaptation. This has further reduced the flow of overseas nurses into Britain because of the time and costs incurred in funding and undertaking this British-based course.[69] As larger numbers of British-trained nurses begin to seek jobs in the NHS, the Department of Health has also shifted its priority to the retention of trained staff, including those from overseas.

Unlike for overseas nurses, the tightening of immigration controls in the 1970s and 1980s did not significantly reduce the numbers of overseas doctors coming to Britain. The output of British medical schools continued to fall short of manpower needs in the NHS. The flow of overseas doctors into and out of Britain is not monitored, but estimates from the early 1980s suggest that around one-third of the yearly influx of overseas doctors returned. Nevertheless their continued employment was not accepted uncritically. Aneez Esmail has shown that as early as the 1960s the columns of the *British Medical Journal* (*BMJ*) were regularly filled with letters complaining of the standards of overseas doctors, particularly those of Asian origin.[70] Among the accusations were that overseas doctors possessed low academic credentials and an inadequate understanding and command of English. We shall see later how these criticisms often masked cultural differences rather than language difficulties. The Merrison Report into the regulations in the medical profession, published in 1975, supported these doubts, and questioned the clinical competence and language skills of overseas doctors. The report concluded that overseas doctors posed a serious risk to standards of medical care in Britain, and its findings sparked a complete overhaul of the professional registration of overseas doctors in Britain. Concerns were also fuelled by evidence that significant numbers of white British doctors were continuing to leave the NHS to work abroad, mainly in the United States and Canada.[71]

Interestingly, UK-trained doctors leaving their home country seemed as likely as their BME counterparts entering Britain to encounter prejudice and difficulties in securing prestigious posts in their chosen country. In their study of physician migration between 1960 and 1979, Wright, Flis and Gupta found evidence of 'a prejudice towards the quality of care provided by foreign medical graduates' across countries.[72] In Britain, many overseas-trained doctors had to accept jobs in unpopular specialties, and in inner-city, or remote rural areas. In Canada, many foreign-trained doctors could only obtain posts in undesirable remote and rural communities. Over the next decades these divisions sharpened until by the 1980s there were few opportunities for foreign-trained medical graduates in wealthy Canadian provinces such as Ontario, whereas the less popular provinces of Newfoundland and Saskatchewan continued to recruit doctors from South Africa and South Asia.[73] Discrimination against migrant doctors, it seems, was not unique to British medicine.

In 1985 the work permit scheme was eventually extended to include doctors. An official 'loop hole' was created however which meant that overseas doctors could continue to seek postgraduate training in Britain for a four year permit-free period, extendable for a further year after approval from the postgraduate dean. In 1997, this permit-free period of postgraduate training was extended to six years. Overseas doctors remained a notable feature of the NHS over the final decades of the twentieth century. In 1997, 44% of 7,229 newly registered doctors (under full registration) had received their initial medical education in non-British countries.[74]

A rise in the output from British medical schools as a result of measures to increase admissions brought about a change in attitude towards the employment of overseas medical graduates. By 2005 the government feared that the recruitment of overseas doctors (non-European Economic Area, EEA) would deny employment to a large number of home-grown medical graduates, especially as international medical graduates (IMGs), who were often highly skilled, and with several years' experience in their chosen field, remained an attractive prospect for the NHS. In a bid to keep junior posts open for graduates who were British or EEA nationals, in April 2006, the Department of Health retrospectively sought to debar IMGs from applying for training posts in the NHS. Under new rules, hospitals were told they must prove they could not recruit a junior doctor from Britain or the EU before shortlisting candidates from other countries. BAPIO (the British Association of Physicians of Indian

Origin) challenged the Government in the High Court, who ruled that the Department of Health's guideline was illegal. The judgement was upheld by the House of Lords in April 2008, but not before thousands of overseas doctors had had their opportunity of permit-free training abruptly withdrawn at great personal and financial costs to themselves and their careers.[75] Currently there are predictions of a shortfall in General Practitioners and again the likely recourse will be to recruit from other countries.

Overview

This chapter has outlined the complex relations between the creation of the NHS in 1948 and its increasing manpower requirements, in the context of post-war labour shortages and mass immigration. It has shown how health workforce crises have been perennial problems in Britain since the 1930s. Shortages of nurses and doctors have arisen because of a range of factors including the difficulties around the recruitment and retention of nurses, the problems in balancing medical manpower supply and demand, and the emigration of UK-trained doctors. Successive governments have used mass-scale recruitment of nurses from the West Indies and Africa, and doctors from South Asia, supplemented by UK-based campaigns to recruit nurses. From the mid-twentieth century, healthcare workers emerged as an international workforce which continues to bring challenges for governments in managing health workforce planning.

We have also begun to discuss the wider context of racism in Britain against which discrimination against overseas clinicians within the NHS must be read. Migrants have influenced every aspect of British life, and Britain has undoubtedly benefited enormously, both economically and culturally. This diversity has not however developed unchallenged. The NHS was not averse to using (and abusing) immigration controls to its advantage and later chapters will reveal evidence of the ways in which institutional racism adversely affected training and career progression of BME clinicians. We also found evidence that some UK-trained doctors who emigrated experienced prejudice and difficulties in gaining jobs in popular locations. Discrimination, it seems, is a common problem across continents and communities.

We turn now to explore how these issues were configured in Manchester. How has the NHS in Manchester tackled recurrent labour shortages? What impact has post-war immigration had on the city and its health services? And how have BME clinicians recruited to Manchester faired against this local backdrop?

Multi-Cultural Manchester

By the time that many overseas nurses and doctors arrived in Manchester after the Second World War, the city's population was already mixed. Ever since the mid-eighteenth century, when Manchester began to grow and prosper as a regional capital, the city has provided homes and workplaces for a multiplicity of nationalities and ethnic groups. Migration patterns in Manchester generally followed those for Britain as a whole. In the eighteenth and early nineteenth centuries, mercantile migrants and those with connections to the textile trade began to settle in Manchester. These included, from the late eighteenth century, Jews from Central and Eastern Europe who made their living as peddlers, hawkers, shopkeepers and export merchants, and from the early nineteenth century, cotton merchants from Germany and Holland, Greek traders, and Armenian silk-merchants.[1] Other European settlers at this time included a small population of Italian artisans who traded in the Market Street area of the city.[2]

The Irish population in Manchester increased especially rapidly in the early nineteenth century. This was partly due to the Irish fleeing Ireland after the failure of the 1798 rebellion against British rule, and also because of Irish handloom weavers seeking work in Manchester's booming cotton industry.[3] The Great Famine of the 1840s increased the Irish presence in Manchester. By 1851, the Irish comprised 15% of the city's population.[4] Many Irish men found low-paid work in the construction industry, working as labourers, builders and 'navvies', building Manchester's canals, railways and roads. They were also heavily employed at Smithfield Market as stallholders, labourers, and porters.[5] Irish women often found work in domestic service or the factories. Most Irish inhabitants of Manchester lived in extreme poverty, in squalid, overcrowded cellar dwellings in the Ancoats district of the city or in Chorlton or Medlock, known as 'Little Ireland'.[6]

In 1851 there were approximately 1,500 Jews in Manchester. Most were shopkeepers and merchants of German or Sephardi (Spanish or Portuguese) origin.[7] In the later nineteenth century, with migration from Eastern Europe, Manchester's Jewish population rose to 35,000 by 1914, making it England's largest Jewish community outside London.[8] Fleeing poverty and persecution in their homelands of the Russian and Prussian Empires, these newcomers were much poorer than their predecessors. Like the Irish, they accepted low-paid work, mainly in tailoring workshops manufacturing cheap clothing. They too lived in densely populated slum districts, such as Red Bank, Strangeways and Lower Broughton, close to their places of work. They were also close to the established Jewish Quarter at Cheetham Hill.[9] As the nineteenth century progressed, upwardly mobile families began to migrate to more desirable areas of the city, such as Cheetham Hill or to the suburbs, such as Higher Broughton in the north, and to Withington and Didsbury in the south.[10]

Between the end of the nineteenth century and the beginning of the First World War, Manchester's multi-ethnic population expanded still further. Italians, mainly from Italy's impoverished deep south, settled in the city in increasing numbers between 1880 and 1914. Many first pursued occupations as street vendors (e.g. street musicians) and as general labourers, later shifting to ice cream vending and manufacturing.[11] Chinese migrants, mainly Cantonese, also settled in the city from the early 1900s, and were employed in the city's laundries. This period also witnessed the formation of Manchester's black community, when West African seamen began settling in the city. A black presence in Manchester expanded in the inter-war period including professionals and students on the one hand, and on the other, West African and West Indian seaman plus other workers and their families.[12] By 1951, there were already 350 Caribbean people living in Manchester.[13] There is also evidence of an Asian presence in Manchester during the 1930s. This mainly consisted of Punjabi traders, who peddled their wares door-to-door.[14] African and Asian restaurants also began to appear at this time, probably catering for migrant sailors and students. Prominent examples were those of Ras Tefari Makonnen, a leading Pan-Africanist radical who moved to the city in the 1930s. He owned a chain of restaurants including the Ethiopian Teashop, the Cosmopolitan, the Orient, a club called the Forum, and a place called Belle Etoile.[15]

During World War Two Manchester played host to refugees from Central Europe, among them Jews and Poles, many of whom chose to stay after the war. The polish 'emigracja', mainly drawn from exiled government members and the Polish Armed Forces, formed the core of Polish communities in Britain after 1945, including

Manchester. As we have already noted, displaced persons from across Europe were brought to Manchester as part of migrant labour schemes in the late 1940s. Western Ukrainians and Belarusians also settled in Manchester after the War. Other migrants to arrive in the 1950s included Chinese, mainly Hakkanese people, forced from their land in the new territories of Hong Kong; Hungarians fleeing the repercussions of the failed uprising against Soviet control in 1956; and Greek Cypriots, following the anti-Greek pogroms in present-day Istanbul.

The major flows of post-war immigration into Manchester, and those which are of direct concern to this study, came however from the West Indies, West Africa, and South Asia. Of the 1.6 million people who left the West Indies between 1955 and 1961, 148,369 (or 9%) came to Britain; of these 9%, nearly 2% came to Manchester.[16] Between 1951 and 1981, the number of Manchester residents born in the Caribbean rose from 351 to 6,263.[17] The majority (4,738) had been born in Jamaica. The rest originated from Barbados, Trinidad and Tobago, the West Indies Associated States (including St. Kitts, Nevis, Anguilla and Antigua), other Caribbean Commonwealth Islands, Belize, and Guyana.[18] Many, it seems, chose Manchester as their final destination because they already had connections here.[19] A survey into the employment of West Indians and West Africans in Manchester conducted in the late 1950s revealed that many were employed in a number of the city's chief industries including engineering, clothing, textiles, building, rubber, woodwork, various miscellaneous factories (hats, materials, chemicals, plastic goods), kitchen work, transport (predominantly road service and maintenance), and other central and local government undertakings.[20] Though many migrants undoubtedly arrived as skilled workers, much of the work they obtained was unskilled and low-paid. Upon arrival in Manchester, the West Indians settled mainly in the Moss Side district, but others could be found living in Old Trafford, Hulme, and Cheetham.

Migrant workers from the Indian subcontinent also began to arrive in Manchester in substantial numbers after World War Two. Pakistanis were predominant among these migrants (4,975 by 1981 out of a South Asian total of 8,415), but there were also Indians, Bangladeshis, and Sri Lankans, forming a 'complex, segmented diaspora' composing different nationalities, religions (Islam, Hinduism, Sikhism and Christianity), languages and regional popular cultures.[21] The initial migration into Lancashire was of single young men who settled in northern towns around Manchester and worked in the ailing cotton mills. The city itself, however, with its tradition of business and commerce, also provided entrepreneurial opportunities. Business niches developed in ethnic grocery food, restaurants, and South Asian fabric shops and travel agents.[22] Building on the work of pre-war, small-scale peddler migrants, many Pakistanis, (Muslims and Hindus from East and West Punjab, who were literate and relatively well-educated) turned especially quickly from factory-wage employment to trading and wholesale in the 1950s. By the 1970s, many moved into the manufacturing of clothing, taking advantage of the inner-city warehouses and workshops left empty by a collapsing textile industry.[23] Students, doctors recruited to the NHS, and other professionals formed a second cohort of South Asians in Manchester. The Asian community predominantly settled in Longsight, Rusholme, Cheetham, Hulme and Whalley Range.

By the 1980s then Manchester's population consisted of an incredibly diverse ethnic mix thanks largely to immigration not only from the New Commonwealth and South Asia, but also the Far East (Hong Kong, Malaysia and Singapore), and East Africa (Kenya, Malawi, Tanzania, Uganda and Zambia). In 1981, West Indians and Pakistanis however formed the largest non-white ethnic groups in the city, (the largest minority ethnic group being the Irish).[24] According to the 1991 Census, 12.6% of Manchester's population were part of a non-white ethnic group (Indian/Pakistani/Bangladeshi, 5.4%; Black groups, 4.7%; Chinese and other groups, 2.6%).[25] Most of these communities were concentrated in the inner city. Manchester's inner-city population had been in decline since the 1930s, paralleled by suburban growth. Manufacturing decline, a policy of re-housing outside the municipal boundary, and the migration of the more affluent to the southern suburbs and several other neighbouring districts intensified this trend in the second half of the twentieth century.[26] As the total inner-city population declined, so the ethnic minority share of the city's population increased. The historical pattern of residential segregation was also preserved, with the poorest, including many of Manchester's ethnic minorities, inhabiting the traditionally impoverished inner city. In the 1980s, the inner-city districts of Manchester contained half the city's total inhabitants, but housed 95% of the West Indian community, and 79% of those from the Indian subcontinent.[27] By the time of the 1991 census, 77% of black and Asian residents lived in thirteen of the city's thirty-three wards. The inner-city wards of Ardwick, Rusholme, Moss Side, Hulme, Whalley Range and Longsight, traditionally wards of high deprivation, had the highest percentages of black and Asian residents.[28]

Post-War Migrants and the Host Community

Manchester, as Peter Fryer notes, has had a mixed history of attitudes to race. Though the city profited from the slave trade it was in the vanguard of support for its abolition in the late eighteenth-century.[29] Evidence suggests that over the centuries foreigners of all origins have received a generally welcome response from their Manchester hosts, although there have also been moments of intolerance and conflict in host/immigrant relations. Minority groups in Manchester have always been vulnerable. In the nineteenth-century the Irish were 'scapegoated for the ills of the 'shock city' of the new industrial society.'[30] At the outbreak of the Second World War, approximately 300 Italians in Manchester were rounded up as 'Enemy Aliens' and interned on the Isle of Man.[31] Meanwhile, anti-Semitism in Manchester has a checkered history.[32]

In defence of their vulnerability, all minority groups in Manchester have through the process of settlement found protection, strength, and identity in the development of institutions (religious, educational, charity), and social, political, and cultural organisations. This was no different for Manchester's black and Asian communities. During the 1930s and 1940s, members of the small black population of Manchester began forming organisations, which reflected not only their concerns with their colonial status but also with the racism they faced. In August 1943, Ras Tefari Makonnen, the Guyana-born restaurateur and nightclub owner, opened the first Negro Welfare Centre in Manchester with the aim 'to help Africans who couldn't carry their own weight'.[33] Also in 1943, the Manchester Negro Association was founded by Dr Peter Milliard, a Manchester-based GP originally from Guyana but who had settled in Manchester in the early 1930s.[34] The Association provided a political and social focus for Manchester's growing black communities, which by now also included a number of West Indians brought into Britain to work in British factories during the war. The Negro Association held monthly meetings at which political issues such as the end of colonial rule in Africa and the Caribbean were discussed.[35]

Manchester became a focal point of Pan-Africanist politics when representatives of the Negro Association helped to establish the UK Pan-African Federation (PAF) in 1944. This was a united front movement which helped coordinate the activities of various African and British-based black organisations. A year later, the fifth Pan-African Congress was held in Chorlton Town Hall.[36] The Congress focused on the problems of colonialism, as well as racism both abroad and in Britain. Addressing the Congress, Dr Milliard, Chair of the PAF, is said to have referred to Manchester's worldwide reputation for 'high liberalism'. He talked of the nineteenth-century efforts of Lancashire cotton-workers who spoke out against slavery, which 'illustrated the hospitality and human understanding of the Lancashire people.' He went on to state his hopes 'that Manchester would continue to merit this high opinion which is held by the Negroes who have lived in the city'.[37]

The remaining records of the Negro Association suggest that Manchester remained central to black politics during the 1950s. As the influx of African-Caribbean migrants increased, the black communities of Manchester came under closer scrutiny, and thus the need for a united front remained. On 9th September 1951, for example, the city hosted a joint meeting of the African Students' Association, the Africa League, and the Negro Association. Among the topics under discussion was the need to counteract the stereo-typical portrayal of black immigrants as users of 'dope', which had reportedly been disseminated in the local press. As well as being portrayed as drug users, African-Caribbean migrants faced other difficulties in the first years of their adjustment. Colour bars, although not officially sanctioned as in the US, affected their access to housing and lodgings, while an informal 'colour tax' meant that many ended up paying inflated rent prices. Much of the housing that was made available to migrants was in a dilapidated condition. They also had to endure discriminatory police surveillance. According to one resident of Moss Side, the local police station had a map indicating the residences of Caribbean people.[38] There was particular local objection to the kind of exuberant cellar parties, or 'shebeens', common to the Caribbean, which apparently did not fit with the 'quiet' culture of Manchester.[39] Such parties often brought arrests by the police, and with them allegations of police brutality, which intensified over the following decade.[40]

By the mid-1950s, studies into the problems associated with immigration, particularly in relation to housing and social adjustment had begun to appear. Janet Reid at the University of Manchester was unusual in that she investigated issues associated with the industrial employment of West Indian and West African migrants in Manchester in 1956.[41] Her research revealed a mixed picture in employer attitudes to migrant workers, with prejudice, on the one hand, and tolerance on the other. While migrant workers often functioned as a useful stopgap in times of shortage, other enterprising managers had attempted to integrate them into permanent workforces in the city. As was common for the period in which it was written, Reid's work focused on the attitudes of employers of migrant labour rather than the experiences of the migrants themselves. By contrast, a series of five articles that appeared in the *Manchester Evening Chronicle* in June 1958, dealt with the diverse experiences of Manchester's growing immigrant groups, including the West Indians and West Africans of Moss Side, foreign students, Eastern Europeans, young, female continental Europeans, and Indians. Collectively entitled 'Strangers in our Midst', the reporter Barry Cockcroft adopted a generally sympathetic tone to the migrant communities he encountered. He pointed out that the problems, which migrants were often associated with – vice, public disorder, and unemployment – were not of their own making. The articles also recounted sometimes hostile incidents between migrants and members of the host population who seemed to be 'distrusting' and even 'jealous' of the migrants' skills, and fearful for their own jobs.[42]

Despite the obvious tensions, Manchester escaped the so-called 'race riots' of 1958. While commentators continued to refer to the 'social problems' associated with the most recent migrants at the beginning of the 1960s, there was also some appreciation of the ways in which the 'presence of the coloured races in Manchester had further increased the cosmopolitan nature of the city's population'.[43] Numerous social and cultural organisations were set up by migrant communities both to assist newcomers in adjusting to the city, and to represent the political interests of the migrants, often drawing their impetus from the broader Black political movements in the US and Britain. By the 1960s there were nine informal West Indian associations in and around Moss Side, including The Caribbean Federal Association, The Colonial Sports and Social Club, The Jamaican Circle, The Trinidad and Tobago Society, The Jamaican Association, The Leeward Islands Peoples' Association, The British Coloured Association, The West Indian National Association, and The British Society for Coloured Welfare.[44] These West Indian organisations represented a somewhat disparate and incoherent collection of social, economic, and political interests, and socialisation occurred within rather than across the various organisations. West Indian students and professionals also tended not to associate with the more politicised organisations; trends which mirrored the socio-economic divisions within the West Indian population in Moss Side itself.[45]

Representing sectors of the Asian community were The Pakistan Society, and the Jamiat-ul-Muslimeen Islamic Cultural Centre (who would later be responsible for commencing work on a purpose built mosque in Victoria Park in 1973). Another organisation was the Pakistani Welfare and Information Centre, set up by local Pakistani business owners in the early 1960s as a welfare agency dealing with the social problems of Pakistani migrants. It was, at that time, the only body to have a recognised office and to employ trained social workers for this purpose. The services provided by the Centre were made available to not just the Pakistani community but to other immigrant groups in the city as well as the English population. A report to the Town Clerk revealed that the centre was indeed used by people of all races, and by statutory and voluntary organisations on behalf of their clients, including the Family Planning Association and Lancashire County Council.[46] In 1965, the Centre enlisted the support of two Pakistani doctors and five lay persons to act as translators between clients and doctors.[47] Another was the Indian Association, which began in the 1950s as regular get-togethers of local Indians and Indian students to celebrate important dates in the Indian calendar, and to share food and music in each others' homes. As the Association grew in size, permanent premises were established. In March 1969, Ghandi Hall (on Brunswick Road in Withington) was officially opened and it became the site of all important Indian functions in the city, as well as being used by a variety of different Indian social and cultural groups.[48]

The mid-1960s saw the emergence of 'race relations' in Manchester. An International Council of Manchester and District (an affiliation of the National Council for the Welfare of Commonwealth Immigrants, and sponsored by Manchester and Salford Council of Social Service and the International Centre) had been set up in 1963. The International Council had limited powers and did not prove particularly effective in dealing with ethnic minority issues.[49] As a result, there were soon calls for greater representation of immigrants across the north west.[50] In 1966 the Manchester Council for Community Relations was set-up in partnership between the Home Office, Manchester City Council and local ethnic minority communities. As a local community-relations council its primary function was to address the issue of immigration and the settlement of black and Asian migrants into Manchester. Over time, it also began to deal with the issues of racism and racial discrimination. Following the first Race Relations Act in 1965, conciliation committees were formed to promote compliance with the Act and to mediate any local conflicts that arose. As a member of the North West Conciliation Committee, Satya Chatterjee, one of our interviewees, remembers going around various hotels and public houses ensuring that new migrants from the new Commonwealth were not discriminated against on the basis of race and colour.[51]

With the tightening of immigration controls it is no surprise that the Manchester area also became the site for over seventy anti-deportation and immigration campaigns and rallies between the 1970s and the 1990s. The first was that of Nasira Begum, who after leaving her abusive husband in 1971 was threatened with deportation by the British government who denied her settlement application on the grounds that she had married out of convenience and that the marriage had been illegitimate. Begum refuted the government's objections, and following a successful campaign in her name was granted the right to stay in Britain in 1981. Many more cases followed. Manchester was home to a number of anti-fascist organizations: the Anti-Nazi League, the North Manchester Campaign Against Racism, Democratic Defence, the Manchester Anti-fascist Committee, the Longsight branch of the Campaign Against Racism and Fascism. Together with local lawyers, most notably Steve Cohen, and activists from left-wing parties and the Asian Youth Movement, these groups presented a united front in fighting state racism in terms of immigration laws.[52]

In July 1981 Moss Side witnessed four days of social disturbances. The riots, which also took place in cities such as Bristol, Birmingham, London, and Liverpool, though not strictly racially motivated were an expression of over twenty years of frustration and anger at racism, discrimination, poverty, and oppressive policing in the inner city, especially the erratic use of 'stop and search' powers and illegal detentions of young people. Moss Side police station was reportedly besieged by 1,000 black and white youths; property and businesses were destroyed by looting and fire.[53] An official inquiry into the disturbances by Lord Scarman blamed them on discrimination, unemployment, and poverty but rejected any notion that institutional racism might also have been a contributory factor.[54] While the riots led to efforts to regenerate Moss Side, the area retained a problematic reputation for crime and violence through the 1980s and 1990s. Problems with racial violence across the city also continued, with incidents such as the murder of thirteen-year-old Ahmed Iqbal Ullah in a racist attack at Burnage high school in 1986. By the 1980s, racism was at its peak in Manchester and in other parts of Britain and had slowly escalated since the mass immigration of workers from the Commonwealth several decades earlier.

During the 1980s and 1990s there were some positive developments for Manchester's ethnic minorities, particularly in the area of health services. In 1986, the Manchester Action Committee on Health Care for Ethnic Minorities (MACHEM) was established. Its mission was to promote equity and eliminate discrimination on grounds of race or religion across all health, social and community services, as well as employment in these sectors, and it had some success in tackling the issues of mental health, diabetes, catering, and facilities to meet religious requirements.[55] Carol Baxter, one of our interviewees, was its Chair. Organisations addressing specific issues within a particular minority community were also established. In 1988, Dr Charan Das Bhagabat, a Geriatric Consultant originally from India, founded the Indian Senior Citizens Centre. Based in Withington, the day centre continues to help lonely, isolated, depressed and disadvantaged elders of the Indian community, providing them with mental, physical, and health improvement.[56] Over the last few decades, health and community-based services designed specifically for Manchester's ethnic minorities have also emerged. These have included translation services, health centres (e.g. Chinese Health Information Centre; the Sickle Cell and Thalassaemia Centre), and various agencies and charities (e.g. the Black Health Agency; the African and Caribbean Mental Health Service). Many of these services have, of course, depended on the input of BME clinicians and we turn now to the experiences of BME nurses in Manchester's health services.

Recruitment of Overseas Nurses

Wartime shortages of qualified nurses and nurse-trainees were not a new problem for Manchester's hospitals. In 1918, for instance, the Royal Infirmary, St Mary's, Ancoats, and Salford hospitals had all reported depleted staffs, particularly in domestic service.[57] During the Second World War, Manchester's hospital services struggled to attract the 300 to 400 student nurses it needed each year, because of the attraction of other sorts of war work. By May 1945, the city's municipal hospitals had a shortage of 219 nurses and 111 domestic staff, a deficiency that resulted in long waiting lists for admissions.[58] The problem of recruitment continued after the creation of the NHS. Throughout the 1950s, local newspapers reported on the long waiting lists and ward closures that resulted from the shortage of nursing staff in the city.[59] In some institutions, such as Crumpsall Hospital, the numbers of nursing staff were nearly 50% below that required.[60] Nursing shortages were common to all of Manchester's NHS institutions, but it was the city's sanatoria, and mental and isolation hospitals that experienced the most chronic staffing deficiencies.[61]

Local campaigns were launched to tackle recruitment problems, particularly in the mental and mental deficiency hospitals. In the early 1950s, for example, Prestwich and Springfield hospitals launched recruitment campaigns involving press and cinema advertisements, posters and leaflets to attract trainees from the local area. An 'open evening' secured the engagement of sixteen new students at one hospital, and there was hope that unemployment in the local cotton industry would increase their number in due course. They also started cadet schemes whereby they hoped to encourage a supply of student nurses.[62] Such efforts, however, generally proved unsuccessful. Reasons given for the shortage of nurses included the attraction of other sorts of work, the poor pay and conditions under which nurses trained and worked, and the fact that trainees were attracted away from Manchester to the larger hospitals in London.

In Manchester, as elsewhere in Britain, overseas labour was used to offset the shortage of trained staff. The employment of foreign labour in Manchester's health services was not a new practice. Irish nurses, for example, had long been recruited to work in Manchester hospitals, and as the Second World War loomed, the Manchester Public Health Committee agreed to employ a limited number of foreign refugees in each of its municipal hospitals, either as trained nurses or for training as nurses.[63] There is, however, no statistical record of the numbers of nurses recruited to train and work in Manchester from overseas in the decades before and after 1945. As overseas nurses could be recruited directly by hospitals or through government-sponsored schemes, it is virtually impossible to track the flow of trainees in the city. Newly qualified nurses often moved around the country as they entered employment, or undertook further training in midwifery and health visiting. Ethnic monitoring is a recent intervention, and the NHS has never kept a record of the number of overseas workers it employs. The evidence of overseas nurses working in Manchester is thereby fragmentary and anecdotal.

Manchester was among one of the first hospital regions to receive domestic workers recruited from overseas after the Second World War. Under the 'Baltic Cygnet Scheme', launched in 1946, young Latvian women were employed at Withington Hospital as domestic maids.[64] Then, in October 1949, as part of a government co-ordinated scheme designed to fill vacancies across the country, Manchester took on six women from Barbados as nursing auxiliaries. Four were dispatched to the Manchester Royal Infirmary (MRI), where they were put to work as ward maids. Another two were taken on at Ancoats Hospital, one as a pantry maid, the other a children's ward maid. The chief nursing authorities at the MRI were dubious about employing these women: 'it was a committee decision not to take coloured girls on the nursing staff'.[65] Their employment was experimental, and subject to them being 'willing to do ward work including scrubbing and polishing of floors'. The Matron of the MRI, Miss Duff-Grant, also warned that 'should a suitable English girl present herself for employment she would be taken'.[66]

The Barbadian authorities paid the women's passage to Britain up front; this was later repaid through weekly wage deductions of five shillings. A report on the placement of these women in Manchester states that all had settled into their new employment. Both hospitals found the women to be 'good workers, punctual and obedient', and said they would be willing to take further recruits, although more time would be required before they could give an opinion as to their upgrading from domestics. Ministry of Health records show that none of the women remained in Manchester. By 1951 all six of the Manchester recruits had moved to other hospitals in the Greater Manchester area and beyond, some as domestics or nurse orderlies, others to commence training as student nurses. By 1954, most of them had returned to Barbados.[67]

Manchester's mental and mental deficiency hospitals, which experienced the most acute shortages of nurses, also relied on the employment of foreign staff.[68] As we have noted, it was to such hospitals that many of those first recruited through European migrant labour schemes were deployed. In 1951, for example, Calderstones Hospital, then governed by the Manchester Regional Hospital Board, had twenty-eight French women who had English classes before entering preliminary training.[69] A report on overseas students in *The Guardian* in 1962 stated that there were an estimated 300 overseas student nurses in Manchester, in hospitals spread all over the conurbation, including North Manchester (54), South and Central Manchester (59), Salford (35), Oldham (35), Ashton-under-Lyne (38), and Stockport (61).[70] Unfortunately, the report does not tell us from where these students originated, on which courses they were enrolled, in which hospitals they were employed, or how many of them remained in Manchester after qualification.

Recruitment of Overseas Doctors

Following the creation of the NHS, the North West suffered most severely of all regions from a shortage of trained medical personnel, including both doctors and dentists. A report in *The Guardian* in 1961, blamed this on the unpopularity of Northern industrial areas among newly qualified doctors who frequently sought practices in the South of England. Though the Medical Practitioners' Committee sought to ration doctors' practices, the ratio of patients to practitioners in many parts of Lancashire was considered too high. Manchester was reported to have six "under-doctored" areas. Due to deaths and resignations, the number of general dental practitioners in the city had reduced from about 200 to 130 since the start of the NHS. Their surgeries had not been taken over, and as a result practices had disappeared.[71]

Manchester Medical School also struggled to supply local demand. Following the Willink Committee's proposal for a 10% reduction in student admissions, the Manchester medical school declined from a total of 662 students in 1953–1954 to 528 in 1960–1961. Annual intakes into the pre-clinical school dwindled to between eighty and eighty-five students in the late 1950s.[72] In 1968, the Todd Committee on Medical Education finally recommended increasing numbers of medical students by enlarging existing medical schools. That same year, the planned expansion of the Manchester Medical School, with new buildings and the development of teaching hospitals at Withington and Hope hospitals, ensured an increase in the annual intake of medical students from 100 to 160.[73] Even so, the Manchester hospitals were reportedly losing many local graduates each year. We saw earlier how significant proportions of newly qualified British graduates emigrated during this period. In the mid-1960s, it was thought that around 25% of doctors who graduated in the North West were taking up posts abroad because of poor pay and conditions in the NHS. This was lower than the national average, which was estimated to be between 30 and 50%.[74]

Within twelve years of the creation of the NHS, Manchester was growing increasingly reliant on overseas junior staff for the day-to-day running of its hospitals, while doctors from India and Pakistan were shoring up the city's GP and dental practices. In 1960 between 30 and 40% of junior medical staff were estimated to be from overseas but there was significant differentiation across specialties and locations with most overseas doctors clustered in unpopular specialties in deprived urban areas, or remote rural areas. Of the 634 registrars and hospital doctors in the Manchester region by February 1960, 329 were British graduates, 59 were from the Irish Republic, and 246 were from overseas.[75] By 1961, it was reported that overseas staff filled about 39% of the junior medical posts in both the Manchester and Liverpool Regional Hospital Board areas. A spokesman for the Boards was quoted as saying that 'their hospitals would be unable to operate without foreign doctors.'[76] In the same year, an investigation by *The Daily Mirror* stated that in Manchester, Leeds and Newcastle, one in every two doctors in Manchester 'are coloured'.[77] Hospitals in the Bury, Oldham, and Rochdale area were said to be staffed up to 70% by

Indian, Pakistani and African graduates.[78] By 1972, more than 80% of all senior house officers working in the Manchester Regional Hospital Board's area were reportedly from overseas, mainly the Commonwealth.[79] We know very little about how these doctors were recruited to work in Manchester, such as whether they were recruited directly from overseas or whether they applied for posts upon their arrival. What we do know is that these BME doctors together with BME nurses contributed significantly to Manchester's multi-racial workforce.

Manchester in the 2000s

In the twenty-first century, the ethnic-makeup of Manchester's population continues to change. As figure 3.1 shows, non-white ethnic groups (including those from mixed backgrounds) now make up just over 23% of the city's total resident population. This marks a rise from 12.6% in 1991 and 19% in 2001. Pakistanis are the largest individual ethnic minority group in Manchester, followed by black Africans.[80]

The new century has seen the arrival of several other migrant groups in Manchester, many of them refugees, from the former Yugoslavia (e.g. Kosovans, Bosnians), Africa (e.g. Congolese, Sudanese, Somalians, Dafur, Sierra Leoneans), and the Middle East (e.g. Iraqis, Libyans). According to the 2001 Census, 14.8% of Manchester residents were born outside Britain, compared with just 9.2% of the population in England as a whole.[81] The largest increases in

Figure 3.1   Proportion of ethnic groups in Manchester in 2008

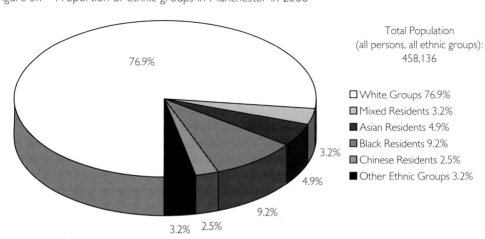

Total Population
(all persons, all ethnic groups):
458,136

☐ White Groups 76.9%
☐ Mixed Residents 3.2%
■ Asian Residents 4.9%
▨ Black Residents 9.2%
▨ Chinese Residents 2.5%
■ Other Ethnic Groups 3.2%

Source: Manchester City Council, 'Manchester Fact Sheet', Summer 2008.

Manchester's BME population were recorded in the black African, Chinese and other white groups, reflecting migration from both African countries such as Nigeria and the new EU accession states, as well as the relative youth of Manchester's Chinese population, reinforced by the large number of students in the city.[82]

A decrease in the total population of Manchester over time means that the BME share of the city's population has increased. In terms of residential distribution, BME groups in Manchester continue to be concentrated in the impoverished inner-city wards. In 2006, the largest proportions of non-white ethnic groups (including those from mixed backgrounds) were found in Longsight, Moss Side, Cheetham, and Whalley Range. Black groups are most likely to be living in Moss Side and Hulme, while Asian groups tend to live in Longsight, Whalley Range, and Cheetham – reflecting historical patterns of settlement among post-1950 migrant groups.[83]

Table 3.1 shows the percentage of staff from minority ethnic groups working throughout the NHS Trusts in Manchester [a more detailed breakdown can be seen in the Appendix]. The figures relating to 'total minority ethnic groups' in this table exclude all white groups, including white Irish and white Europeans, as well as those not declared. The figures for those Trusts serving the City of Manchester fall well below the percentage of non-white groups in the city as a whole (see figure 3.1).

The total figures for minority ethnic groups are in some cases much lower than those officially stated by the Trusts in their annual workforce reports. For example, in their 2008/2009 workforce planning report, Manchester NHS declared that staff from minority ethnic groups make up approximately 18.4% of the workforce, equating to 475 employees from a total workforce of 2577. As we can see, this figure is far higher than that shown in table 3.1. The figure of 18.4% can only be obtained if all ethnic groups excluding white British are counted, as well as those not declared. The figures quoted by the Trusts on their respective websites are shown in table 3.2.

Closer scrutiny of specific staff groups within NHS Trusts in Manchester reveals that BME communities are under-represented in executive, senior professional and support worker positions. [See Appendix for a full breakdown of workforce ethnicity by staff group]. The most ethnically diverse staff groups tend to be those in the medical and dental fields. There are also differences between the Trusts. BME staff are also underrepresented at senior levels of NHS organisations in Manchester. Among Trust Board members at the Pennine Acute Trust, for example, BME members make up 14.3% of Non-Executives and 0.0% of Executives. Figure 3.2 shows

Table 3.1   Ethnic audit of staff at key Manchester NHS organisations

Ethnic Group	Manchester NHS		Central Manchester University Hospitals		University Hospital South Manchester		Pennine Acute Trust (Sept 2008)		Manchester Mental Health Trust (excluding bank staff)	
	Headcount	%	Headcount	%	Headcount	%	Headcount	%	Headcount	%
White	2207	86.29	7124	78.9	3915	83.2	1465	85.9	1116	74.85
Mixed	51	2.03	126	1.4	43	0.9	9	1.0	27	1.81
Asian	111	4.36	794	8.7	361	7.7	30	8.0	54	3.62
Black	70	2.71	353	3.9	100	2.1	14	1.7	77	5.16
Chinese	10	0.40	55	0.6	20	0.4	0	0.4	4	0.27
Other ethnic groups	30	1.17	137	1.5	52	1.1	5	1.3	8	0.54
Not stated	78	3.04	440	4.9	214	4.5	28	1.7	205	
Total minority ethnic group (excluding all white groups) and not stated	272	10.67	1,465	16.1	576	12.2	58	12.4	170	11.4

Source: Data provided by NHS Trusts under Freedom of Information.

Table 3.2 Most recent percentage of 'BME', 'ethnic minority', 'non-white', or 'non-white British' staff at four Manchester NHS Trusts as defined and stated by those Trusts

	Manchester NHS	Central Manchester University Hospitals	University Hospital South Manchester	Pennine Acute Trust (Sept 2008)
Total minority ethnic groups as stated by Trusts	18.4% (BME)	20.1% (ethnic-minority backgrounds)	12.3% (non-white)	15.1% (non-white British backgrounds)
Average ethnic minority population in area served by Trust	23.1% (local Manchester population, other ethnic groups) (*Source*: 2006 ONS experimental population estimates)	25.5% (City of Manchester); 39.6% (Central Manchester) (*Source*: 2001 Census)	6.7% (Wythenshawe population)	12.6% (includes Manchester, Rochdale, Bury and Oldham) (*Source*: 2001 Census)

Source: NHS Trust websites.

the number of staff in senior management posts by their ethnicity for some other Manchester NHS Trusts.

The NHS in Manchester has notably remained reliant on overseas recruitment. Between 2000 and 2002, Manchester Royal

Figure 3.2 Headcount of senior management posts in three Manchester NHS Trusts by ethnic group, 2009 (headcounts shown above bars).

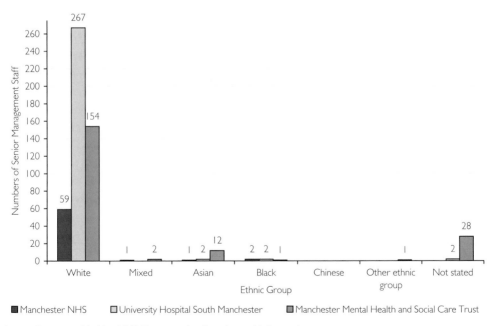

Source: Data provided by NHS Trusts under Freedom of Information.

Infirmary recruited more than 250 nurses from India. The then head of nursing at the MRI, argued that without the recruits almost twenty wards would had to have closed. At that time, Indian nurses accounted for one in ten of the Infirmary's nursing workforce, which also included international nurses from the Philippines, Australia, Spain, Ghana, Germany, Iceland, and the Yemen.[84] Since 2004, Irish nurses have once again been recruited to work in Manchester's hospitals, encouraged by higher salaries and incentives such as subsidised flights home.[85]

In the final decades of the twentieth century significant numbers of graduate doctors from South Asia and Africa continued to fill junior positions in the region's health services (some of our respondents among them). The tightening of immigration controls has inevitably made this recruitment more difficult in the long-term. Meanwhile, the retirement of those Asian doctors who came to Britain in the 1950s and 1960s has threatened to leave huge gaps in the service, particularly in general practice. In the Greater Manchester region alone, some 40% of Asian doctors were expected to retire between 2003 and 2007.[86] In response, the government and local health authorities have in recent years sought other sources of overseas labour. In 2001 a pilot project funded by the Department of Health resulted in the recruitment of up to twenty Spanish doctors, employed on two-year contracts, to GP practices across Liverpool and Manchester.[87]

Table 3.3   Ethnicity of nurses, midwives and health visitors employed in Manchester NHS Trusts

Ethnic Group	Manchester NHS	Central Manchester University Hospitals	University Hospital South Manchester	Pennine Acute Trust (Sept 2008)	Manchester Mental Health Trust (excluding bank staff)
White	89.42%	76.0%	78.7%	86.3%	77.51%
Mixed	1.32%	0.9%	1.3%	1.1%	2.01%
Asian	2.04%	13.8%	10.7%	6.5%	1.46%
Black	2.28%	3.3%	3.5%	2.6%	7.50%
Chinese	0.12%	0.4%	0.6%	0.2%	0.55%
Other ethnic groups	0.72%	0.5%	1.2%	1.2%	0.18%
Not stated	4.1%	4.9%	4.1%	2.1%	10.79%
Total minority ethnic groups (%)	6.48%	18.9%	17.3%	11.6%	11.7%

Source: Data provided by NHS Trusts under Freedom of Information.

Table 3.4   Ethnicity of medical and dental staff employed in Manchester NHS Trusts

Ethnic Group	Manchester NHS	Central Manchester University Hospitals	University Hospital South Manchester	Pennine Acute Trust (Sept 2008)	Manchester Mental Health Trust (excluding bank staff)
White	62.50%	57.9%	64.4%	44.3%	46.43%
Mixed	1.04%	8.2%	1.4%	2.6%	3.57%
Asian	21.88%	26.1%	23.9%	37.7%	23.21%
Black	0.00%	2.8%	1.7%	3.8%	7.14%
Chinese	2.08%	3.0%	1.5%	2.3%	0.00%
Other ethnic groups	5.20%	2.5%	4.4%	6.7%	3.57%
Not stated	7.29%	5.8%	2.7%	2.6%	16.08%
Total minority ethnic groups (%)	30.2%	42.6%	32.9%	53.1%	37.49%

Source: Data provided by NHS Trusts under Freedom of Information.

Tables 3.3 and 3.4 show the percentages of nursing and midwifery, and medical and dental staff by ethnic group employed in Manchester NHS Trusts 2008/2009. As can be seen, there is considerable variation among the various Manchester NHS Trusts, and between these NHS Trusts and national figures shown in table 3.5.

Table 3.5   Ethnicity of qualified nursing, midwifery and health visiting staff, and medical and dental staff in Britain (2008/2009)

	Qualified Nursing, Midwifery and Health Visiting Staff	Medical and Dental Staff of all countries of qualification (within hospital and community health services (HCHS))
Total minority ethnic groups (%)	19.2%	40.4%
White	265,123	53,296
Mixed	3,503	2,010
Asian	22,844	25,446
Black	25,199	3,220
Chinese	2,150	1,759
Other ethnic group	9,414	3,723
Unknown[1]	57,879	9,213

[1] Unknown includes un-stated and unrecorded. The ethnic group of all bank staff is unrecorded.
Source: NHS Information Centre.

Future predictions are that Manchester's population is set to rise by 68,000 by 2015. The population within white groups is set to fall from 76.8% in 2006 to 71.9% in 2015, and the population of BME groups set to increase from 23.3% to 28.1% within the same period, with the largest increases projected to be in the city centre and the wards of Ardwick, Hulme, Moss Side, Fallowfield, and Cheetham. The challenge for the NHS in Manchester will be to ensure that it keeps pace with these developments ensuring that in the years to come its workforce is representative of the multi-racial population it serves.

Overview

This chapter has provided the background canvas for exploring the professional experiences of BME clinicians in the city since 1945. While much of the evidence is of a fragmentary nature, we have shown that the NHS in Manchester has throughout its sixty-year history periodically relied on the recruitment of overseas nurses and doctors to fill labour shortages in its hospitals. The handful of individuals in our case studies presented below represent the generations of clinicians from whose work the NHS in Manchester has benefited.

We have also seen that by the time nurse-trainees and junior doctors began to arrive in Manchester from overseas, the city's population was already incredibly ethnically diverse. As part of the wider post-war migration, these nurses and doctors made their unique contribution to the ethnic and racial mix of the city, often playing a hands-on role in developing ethnically-aware services for migrant communities. At the same time, however, the presence of black and Asian nurses and doctors also added to the problems of immigration in the city and beyond. A marked increase in the employment of overseas nurses and doctors at a time of rising xenophobia and opposition to immigration in general, contributed to an increasingly negative climate of opinion towards these two groups of clinicians. In the chapters that follow we will explore how antipathy towards BME doctors and nurses, both from outside and within the two professions, emerged and how these attitudes shaped their experiences of working in the NHS.

Dr Satya Chatterjee (*right*) in his
room at Wythenshawe Hospital,
Manchester; and (*below left*)
with members of the Overseas
Doctors' Association, Dr Venopal
(*below right*) and Dr Karim Admani.

Remi Clarke (neé Allen) (*right*); and in March 1970
receiving her theatre prize from the Bishop of
Hertford (*below*).

Jasmine Edwards as a student nurse.

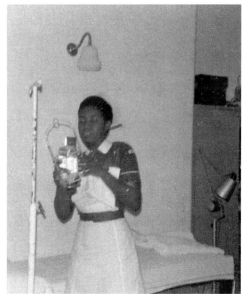

Carol Baxter (*above left*) as a first year student nurse standing outside the Nurses' Home, Hope Hospital, Salford; (*above right*) as a second year student nurse on the paediatric ward, Hope Hospital, Salford.

Health Visitor Neisha Fielder (third from left) with colleagues at Longsight Health Centre, Manchester.

Louise DaCocodia on duty (*above*) and attending a Race Relations Conference, 1976 (*below*). © Greater Manchester County Record Office (These photographs are held by and reproduced with permission from Greater Manchester County Record Office. Refs: DPA 1828/15; DPA 1828/17)

Jannett Creese (*above, on the left of the photograph*) on the wards, Christmas Day, 1960, and receiving the Matron's Prize in 1963 (*below*).

Dr Syed Nayyer Abidi presenting at a health awareness meeting (*above*); and with his publication 'Prevention is Always Better than Cure', the UK's first bilingual (English/Urdu) healthcare book (*below*).

Dr Mahmood Adil receiving his Master of Public Health at the University of Glasgow, 1990 (*left*); and running an immunisation clinic in Maidstone, Kent, where he was paediatrics registrar in 1993 (*below*).

4

Nurses, Midwives and Health Visitors

From the late 1930s to the present day, nurse shortages have been an enduring problem in British health services. The mass recruitment of BME nurses from the late 1940s onwards offered a speedy political resolution of the successive crises although difficulties over nurse recruitment and retention persisted over the period. Low wages, unattractive working conditions, and alternative employment opportunities have all been cited as reasons for recurring nurse shortages in Britain. To understand these apparently intractable problems we have to look at the professionalisation of nursing in the nineteenth century. With its roots in domestic work, nursing emerged as a respectable occupation for the glut of unmarried middle-class girls in the mid-nineteenth century and these workers were encouraged to prize notions of vocation and public service above levels of remuneration. Schools of nursing trained nurses in practical skills rather than medical knowledge and although nursing hierarchies were established and senior staff managed hospital wards and organised nursing work, nurses were ultimately subordinate to doctors and their employers. From the 1880s onwards nurses campaigned for the legal recognition of nursing as a profession although they received little support from GPs who feared competition from nurses over the care of patients at home, or from hospitals which were concerned that a longer training period would compromise their access to trained nurses and limit their powers as employers. The political climate changed after the First World War and in 1919 the Nurses' Registration Act established a framework for registration and regulation through the formation of the General Nursing Council (GNC). Nevertheless, the GNC emerged as a weak body with limited influence over the status of nursing. Witz argues that the consequences of the Registration Act were to constrain nurses within unequal partnerships with the state, hospital employers, and professional relationships with doctors.[1] Since the 1970s, reconfigurations in nurse training, the development of academic nursing, and new posts like nurse-practitioners have improved the status of nursing although levels of nurse remuneration remain considerably lower than those of doctors. The experiences of BME nurses have been shaped by this longer history of nursing and we will see below how the internal hierarchies and structures of nurse training in particular, exacerbated the problems of racism and discrimination.

BME Nurses and Racism

The first wave of BME nurses experienced problems almost as soon as they began their nursing careers in the NHS in the 1950s and there was much discussion around the difficulties created by cultural differences. Communication and language, educational ability, and ignorance of the 'British-way of life' were all seen as presenting a problem to the selection and suitability of overseas nurses in the NHS.[2] Nevertheless, 'the centrality of racism in the way these cultural differences are experienced' was not part of these discussions.[3] It was not until the 1980s that racism emerged as a key factor in the low status and marginality of black and minority ethnic nurses in the NHS. Carol Baxter's study of the black nurse, published in 1988, was the first major piece of work to bring 'to light the extent and nature of racism in nursing and its effect on the employment of black nurses'.[4] Drawing on the 'voices of real people' – 90% of her sample of thirty nurses lived and worked in the Manchester area – Baxter's work exposed the racist underpinnings of the nursing profession.[5] Their findings confirmed that overseas nurses, who were over-represented in the pupil, auxiliary and enrolled grades were widely regarded as a cheap source of labour for the NHS, and that the entire infrastructure of the nursing profession worked to the disadvantage of those whose skin colour was not white. Written at a time of increasingly tough immigration controls and falling recruitment and retention among BME nurses in Britain, Baxter warned that unless action was taken to tackle racism the 'black nurse will become extinct in the National Health Service within the next ten years'.[6] The implications of this loss were profound:

> 'The failure of such a major institution to reflect the multiracial structure of British society would have serious implications for racial harmony and the stability of race relations, and would severely limit the ability of the NHS to appreciate the

needs of, and deliver effective care, to Britain's multiracial population.[7]

Baxter's work sparked further studies in the field.[8] Taken as a whole, this body of research has shown that BME nurses face difficulties at every stage of their careers. Our own interviews identified difficulties in training, in deployment, in nurses' working relationships with patients and colleagues, and in promotion and career development.

Joining the NHS

Our nurse interviewees chose to undertake training in Britain for many reasons including the desire to gain world-recognised professional training and qualification, high prospects of unemployment in their home countries, and the promise of a better future in Britain. Some were driven by a desire to travel and see the world, while for others it was an opportunity to work in the NHS, an institution they had heard so much about. The overseas nurses we spoke to were recruited to the NHS via various routes. Some applied direct to hospitals in Britain; others applied through the government offices of the home country which then passed them on via the consulate to a British hospital.

> *I've always wanted to be a nurse and I left home when I was just twenty, after having applied and got a place at St. Leonard's Hospital in London ... it [the student position] was advertised. I think I got hold of a 'Nursing Times' from somewhere but I can't remember where.* JC

> *I always wanted to travel and to do my nurse training here ... I applied through the British Council and arranged to do my training in Bradford in Yorkshire. I tried to prepare myself by getting as much information as possible. The British Council was helpful by meeting me at the airport and kept in touch afterwards.* JE

> *I came to England at age 18 to do a Public Health Inspection course, but when I got here they told me I needed work experience, which I didn't have; I came straight from school. So I decided to go into nursing.* NF

> *I got really fascinated in the idea of the NHS, and with the transparency with which people discussed the health service. I think that gave me a commitment to want to study in the UK and to understand the NHS healthcare system ... I wanted to expand my horizons and to study abroad, and nursing seemed a particularly attractive option because the*

Government then was recruiting nurses into the UK, so I applied when I finished my A Levels; I applied for one of these nursing scholarships and I got a scholarship to come to study in England. CB

Arrival in Britain brought many changes to the everyday lives of overseas nurse recruits.

When I arrived in London, it didn't meet any of my expectations ... It took me a year to settle. When I got to the hospital, at first ... I said to my cousin, 'that is not a hospital, it's a prison.' ... I found it extremely cold, really, really cold ... The food I found particularly difficult ... I forced myself to eat. JC

I can remember [arriving in Salford] in December 1970, in fact it was New Year's Eve ... so you can imagine it was so different and cold. CB

Adjustment to living in England was facilitated by family already in the country, by other overseas students, and the church. While hospital accommodation for nurses was known to be generally poor at this time, our respondents also spoke of the Nurses' Homes as a home-from-home, which perhaps made settling in that little bit easier.[9]

There was also a very caring sort of atmosphere in the hospital and in the nurses' home; the Matron, and the Deputy Matron, they were like the big boss and you were in awe of them but you felt great respect ... And the Home Sister ... was like your mother; she was just fussing over you if you didn't have your breakfast before you went to work and that sort of thing and it was nice because when I left there I used to write to her; I just missed that atmosphere there. JE

We had a good time because we were very well looked after in the nurses' home ... they don't have nurses' homes now. The matron came and met you, she took you shopping to buy your winter clothes, and you were kind of well looked after. A nice warm bed, a cleaner to clean your room for you, three meals a day in the dining room. CB

Some interviewees were the only black nurses in their training group. Others revelled in multi-racial cohorts.

I was one of four black nurses at the hospital. JE

There were Germans, Mauritians, and people from the Seychelles. It was heavenly. It was absolutely heavenly. People came from all over the UK as well to do this course, from Hastings and from up here. It was just brilliant. MH

Very, very mixed group. From India, from Jamaica, from Africa, so quite a mixed group. RC

Some of those we spoke to fully intended to return home after completion of their training but for personal reasons – marriage and family – they have remained in Britain.

I'd given myself eight years here and that was it, and I've been here since 1954 ... Yes, my intention was to go home. JE

I was born in Nigeria, I'm sixty-three years old, I came to England when I was eighteen, mainly to study nursing really, and I gave myself five years to go back – and I'm still here. RC

Training

One of the identified problem areas facing BME nurses between the 1950s and 1970s was their training. During the large-scale West Indian recruitment campaigns of the 1950s and 1960s, black nurses were frequently and deliberately channelled onto courses leading to the State Enrolled Nurse (SEN) certificate, rather than the State Registered Nurse (SRN) certificate, irrespective of their educational background. The SEN was an inferior qualification, which carried no international recognition. This meant it was of little use to those who wished to return home. As a number of our interviewees pointed out:

I know quite a few people were duped into training for SEN. They did the SEN course but I don't think they knew the difference and that wasn't fair. JC

A lot of girls were misled into believing that they were studying to become SRNs. They didn't know the difference ... you don't have those two levels in the Caribbean. CB

Labelled the 'health service's biggest confidence trick', many recruits discovered too late that the enrolled nurse qualification was virtually useless.[10] This experience was shared by those channelled onto registered mental nurse (RMN) training courses, as they too were not made aware of the difference between this and general nursing.[11]

The segregation created by the two-tier nursing system had a detrimental effect on the subsequent career trajectories of overseas BME recruits, leaving many of them excluded from promotion to higher grades.[12] Those who qualified as SENs faced a long, arduous, and often fruitless battle to gain acceptance to training for the register. Some studies suggest that there may even have been a deliberate policy to prevent SENs, especially those from minority groups, from doing SRN training.[13] In 1986, the United Kingdom Central Council for Nursing and Midwifery (UKCC) announced its Project 2000 proposal to remove the two-tier structure in nursing by phasing out the state enrolled nurse and introducing the three-year Registered Nurse Qualification (RGN). Conversion courses were offered for SENs directly threatened by this move, but acceptance onto these courses required recommendations and references from ward sisters and nurse managers. Accounts of those seeking to convert at this time suggested that the prejudices of their managers might limit their chances of doing so.[14] Furthermore, black nurses remained over-represented in the lower grades.

The nurses we interviewed all originally trained as SRNs/RGNs before pursuing further training in midwifery, health visiting and other fields. Yet, as the following accounts suggest, SRN/RGN status was certainly no guarantee against discrimination in their working lives.

Working in the NHS

Research in the 1980s showed that BME nurses in British hospitals were often assigned the more 'menial, hardest and least rewarding jobs' to do, both during training and after they had qualified.[15] In some cases they were treated as little more than domestics.

> *If I was actually leading the doctors round with the consultant, the consultant would send me off to get a glass of water ... I know that sounds really petty – but ordinarily they'd have asked somebody else to go and get a glass of water.* MH

It is also clear from some of the statements made by those we interviewed that the NHS in Manchester did not have the best record of employing BME staff in skilled posts. A study of the history of Withington hospital, published in 1975, describes how a 'good number' of nursing auxiliaries at that institution, many of them deployed on the geriatric wards, were drawn from the local immigrant communities of Moss Side.[16] One of our interviewees who came to Withington as a Staff Midwife in 1985 described a similar scene.

> *I could see there were a few black doctors ... not just cleaners. Predominantly most of the black staff that [I] came across were cleaners, rather than anything of higher [status].* RC

These problems were not only restricted to Withington.

I was told I was the first black ... health visitor that they'd employed and I thought shame on you, because there must be a lot more. JE

Another nurse described the difficulties she faced in finding a post in Manchester in the mid 1980s.

My friends or colleagues who wanted to move back up, the jobs were there for them, but what I found was that they didn't want me. When I applied, it was almost as if [they were thinking] 'you're an RGN. We're not used to black RGNs.' ... that was the feeling that I got. MH

After two years she got a post at the MRI on the gastroin-testinal ward. While she enjoyed her work she was the '*only black Nurse RGN*' on the ward, and felt 'isolated' and 'constantly under scrutiny'. She later left to work in the community. On returning to the MRI a few years ago, she noticed some definite changes.

I do think things probably have changed [since the 1980s]. I did a return to nursing a year and a half ago at the MRI and my heart was thumping as I was going on the ward ... it did feel different, definitely felt freer, although that could be just because I'm older and I didn't need to be there. But I also felt that there was far more equality and there were far more black RGNs because everyone's an RGN now. I mean many were from African nations so that was good; so it didn't feel like you were the only one. Everybody respected what everybody said. Everyone had the same expectations, the skills ... And in fact most of the ... health care assistants ... weren't all black or all white. It was just a mixture, and it was the same with the cleaners. They were a mixture as well, whereas when I went there [in the 1980s] it was very hierarchical and colour was a definite indication of where you were in the pecking order. MH

The health care assistants referred to here were introduced as a result of Project 2000, when student nurses were removed from hospitals and into universities, and enrolled nurse training was stopped. Health care assistants function as support workers in hospitals performing a significant amount of the service provision previously done by students and qualified nurses. Research suggests that despite Project 2000 a two-tier racialised system of nursing remains in place in Britain. There is still a predominance of black staff as health care assistants, porters and cleaners, and health care assistants find it difficult to become qualified nurses.[17]

Unpopular Specialisms

Another noticeable feature of the experiences of BME nurses in the NHS was their disproportionate deployment in low status specialisms such as geriatrics and mental health. In contrast, they were 'grossly under-represented' in higher status specialisms such as surgery.[18]

> *The black girls for instance, the nurses, were pushed into geriatrics and psychiatry to work, whereas white girls did the more progressive options.* CB

This situation was endorsed during training where BME student nurses were overlooked in favour of their white colleagues for assignment to the more specialised wards such as obstetrics or surgery. This often meant that BME trainee nurses were denied the training and experience necessary to help them progress in their careers.

> *I put my hand up to study obstetrics and ultimately when the list came out I was given geriatrics, all black girls were, and I remember challenging that and asking questions ... I said, 'but you said it was a first come, first served basis?', he [her nurse tutor] said 'no, we didn't say anything of the sort.' People just lied. They did what they wanted to do because they knew that there was no comeback.* CB

> *The ward that I asked for they didn't give me. They gave me the TB ward which I didn't really want to work on because people didn't like injections for TB, it was very painful. There was a very nice Sister on one of the wards and she asked me if I would come and work for her and I said 'yes' but they didn't give me that ward. So I left. I left nursing, yeah, I got a bit disillusioned.* NF

One nurse, who trained as an RGN in London in the 1980s, recalled that her tutor held certain racialised assumptions about the suitability of black nurses for particular nursing roles.

> *Well I find it interesting that a lot of black nurses go into midwifery or onto the community. There weren't that many that stayed in general nursing or in the other sorts of specialisms and I think that's a lot to do with a sort of racism; ... it's like the expectation, a racial expectation that we're good at midwifery ... I remember when I was doing my training ... I wasn't particularly interested in midwifery any more than I was particularly interested in any of the other disciplines, but I remember my tutor saying you'd be a perfect midwife, and all the black nurses were 'midwifery, midwifery, midwifery'. That's pushing us down that path.* MH

Further Training: Midwifery, Health Visiting and Community Nursing

There is also evidence, however, which suggests that BME nurses wishing to work in the community, especially as health visitors, received less favourable treatment than their white colleagues.[19] Some of our interviews revealed that the attitudes of those responsible for selecting nurses for training, as well as the health visitor/community tutors could be biased against both BME nurses and BME clients.

> *I was interviewed in Hyde or Stalybridge for the health visiting before I'd applied at the place in Manchester. It was very late in the academic year when I applied, but they turned me down, I think they asked me about my attitude to black people and so on … I was talking freely you know, but I got turned down for that.* NF

Though she eventually secured a place on health visitor training (after three applications), this nurse continued to experience 'difficulties' with her training supervisors. Previous work has also shown that black nurses felt they were also treated somewhat differently to their white colleagues when it came to interviews for health visitor or community nurse training.[20]

> *I was interviewed by the head of community nursing, and she still asked some strange questions. If somebody didn't want you to go into their house because you were black and all this because it was community-based … I thought, I could ask her how many people she's going to ask the question 'if a black service user doesn't want you in their house, how will you deal with it?'; but I don't think she would have done.* MH

Night Shifts

Night duty was another area in which BME nurses have been found to be disproportionately deployed.[21] Some nurses chose nights because they fitted with childcare responsibilities, offered marginally better pay, and presented BME nurses with one of the few opportunities to gain promotion and job security. According to Baxter's interviewees, nights also offered an escape from the indignities of daytime, where racist remarks and criticisms of their capabilities were more likely to take place. One nurse we interviewed spent much of her career as a Night Sister working alongside black and Irish nurses. In her experience, few English nurses worked the night shifts.

Black people come here. They're young. They get married or not and they have children and night duty was the better option. In the case of English nurses, very, very few of them worked after they got married, and Irish people, they were immigrants; they felt they were immigrants as well, and sometimes they were treated as badly as we were. JC

The introduction of a rotation system has since alleviated some of the discrimination engendered by night shift practice.

Relations with Patients and Colleagues: Day-to-Day Racism

One of the first challenges for newly-arrived BME nurses was adapting to the differences in culture and getting to grips with English slang.

I tell you a funny story; in my culture if someone older than yourself is … telling you off, as a sign of respect you didn't look at them … You had your head bowed … [matron] was telling me off, and I was … looking down. 'Look at me when I'm talking to you', [she said]. And I put my head up and I said, 'But matron, in my culture one isn't allowed to look at the elderly in the face.' … I was just getting in deeper and deeper. I didn't realise that calling her … elderly was actually an insult … When she was telling me off she was actually laughing. RC

I thought I spoke good English until I came to England and all the slang … I remember this woman saying, 'Nurse, I want to spend a penny.' And I went, 'Well it's 6 o'clock Mrs Clark, the shops are closed.' And she kept going on about it, and I knocked on the sister's office and I said, 'Sister, I think Mrs Clark is a bit confused. She keeps saying she wants to spend a penny. I have explained that the shops are closed.' She said, 'Take her to the toilet, quick, before she wets the bed!' Too late, she'd already done it. RC

Even making tea could be stressful. One of our interviewees remembered an incident in 1954 when her Ward Sister was entertaining the junior doctors in her office.

I've never forgotten that cup of tea … the Sister … said 'Nurse will you make some tea and bring it in on a tray'. [so] I … put the tea in the pot and … put the milk in, put everything in this pot. I took it in … I can't remember if I put sugar in or I took the sugar bowl, and she said 'where's the milk?'. I said 'it's in there' … She thought I was bonkers. JE

On the whole, most of those we spoke to stressed the infrequency of personal racist attacks from patients, although when prompted many did recall at least one or two such incidents. Working on the wards, a number had experienced racist insults, such as *'take your black hands off me'*. Others remembered occasions when their abilities and seniority were questioned by patients and their relatives.[22] The health visitors among the sample also recalled occasions when they had been refused entry to peoples' homes because of their West Indian background.

For many, it was the reactions, attitudes and approaches of colleagues that often presented for our interviewees the main source of personal racist attacks and betrayals. As the following examples show, BME nurses could not always rely on the support of their white colleagues in the event of racist attacks from patients.

> *None of the patients have ever been bigoted or rude or dismissive or mistrustful. It was always your colleagues that you felt you got that from.* MH

> *You didn't worry so much because you're there to care for them. It was the staff support for them that was the worst bit … pretending they didn't hear it happen and if you said 'well did you not hear that, can you not say something', they'd say 'well don't be so sensitive'.* CB

> *They [white colleagues] just ignored it and sometimes they even colluded with it. They didn't back you up at all, they just didn't … and it wasn't something you wanted to talk about because you're ashamed.* JC

Personal racist jibes from staff were also not uncommon.

> *I was aware that I was being constantly assessed by some of my colleagues. I found no difficulty with the clients … I can remember a young health visitor coming in, she'd been out visiting and she'd come back and she said 'Oh', she said, 'they're all in their dressing gowns, they're all the same'; she's talking about black people … and then she realised that I was there. Just now and then you'd get that.* JE

> *So I got a job as a health visitor and there were two other health visitors and they were just nitpicking about the tea that I drank — I had blackcurrant tea — and they used to say it stunk … The clinic clerk used to do the hearing test with the health visitors — I'd had training in Stockport, Tameside and then Macclesfield — and then they started criticising my hearing test and then the clerk would make rude remarks about black people and so on.* NF

A feeling of isolation and 'otherness' was expressed by some of the nurses we interviewed.

I wasn't welcome ... I always felt like an outsider. JC

So there were a lot of auxiliary nurses who were black and a fair smattering of enrolled nurses, or SENs, but very, very few registered nurses ... Asian doctors or white doctors couldn't get their head round that at all ... It was ... you're just in the wrong place. You're just not right ... No matter how hard I worked and I feel I was a good nurse – certainly caring, diligent, accurate and safe – I never felt as if I was ... part of the ... inner circle ... I think I'm invisible to these people. That's what I began to think. MH

The nurses we interviewed often faced their problems at work alone. On their own, some issues appeared 'too petty' to merit making a fuss, and as Baxter argues: 'The already precarious position in which the black nurse finds herself does not lend itself to 'rocking the boat''.[23]

I never raised them [issues with colleagues] because I was never sure and I didn't like to admit it. I've never spoken about it before ... saying it out loud makes it more real and more painful. It also seems very petty. Why does it matter if someone doesn't put your name on a flaming Christmas card, for God's sake? But when you see that ... all their names were on except for yours, you ... think oh, what's going on here then. MH

I think there was discrimination, because I think I'm quite outspoken ... I think because maybe people could read my face or maybe because I might have spoken up, I don't know, because that still goes on. I still get into trouble for speaking up. NF

I got on very well with auxiliary nurses who were black, that was it. And they were really supportive as well, really helpful and really kind and even though they'd never say it, when I look back on it, I think to myself maybe they knew something but they weren't saying. MH

Well, for ages and ages I've been going around asking the black nurses, mostly auxiliaries and SENs, to form a black group within the Health Service for black nurses but they were too scared of losing their jobs so I didn't get anywhere. JC

Career Development and Promotion

The individual employment experiences of our nurses in Manchester were, on the whole, positive.

I had the most wonderful time ... as a nurse and health visitor ... In Urmston, Flixton and Davyhulme I worked with a very dedicated staff of health visitors, school nurses, doctors, and administrative staff, and it was just pleasant to go to work. JE

People have been very good, and I get a lot of respect here. NF

A job became available at Withington, again, for a staff midwife, so I thought, I'll go there. [It wasn't] a short-term contract. It was a permanent contract, so I applied and I got the job and I felt at home straight away there; they made me feel welcome. RC

I spent about ten years in Withington. And there you feel that you can develop as much as you can and everybody was supportive ... I represented the night staff on various committees during the day. I went on several courses ... At Withington you had everything. Withington was a big teaching hospital and it had everything to stretch you. JC

Some nurses found differences between the inner-city hospitals of Manchester and outlying institutions. This nurse was a Ward Sister at Stockport Infirmary, before transferring to Manchester.

Instead of covering a group of wards at night ... they put me on one ward, like a Staff Nurse, and I felt that demoted me ... What I was doing I could do it with my eyes closed and they were twenty years behind anyway ... after six months I went to Withington where I think they were more broad-minded. Well, Manchester's inner city, isn't it, and more urban and there were more black people there, not in a Sister's capacity, but ... cleaners and ... patients; my boss ... knew that [I] had to grow and develop to like the job and that is what I got ... I went on so many courses they used to call me 'Minister of Courses'. I enjoyed it. I spent nearly eleven years at Withington and I enjoyed it. JC

As with other industries, however, the nursing profession was reluctant to have black people in positions where they would have to manage and have authority over white workers.

Although they didn't say it, they implied that they didn't want a black person to give them, well she [a colleague] implied ... that, they didn't want a black person to give them orders and we had a few run-ins [she and her colleague] but I just left it at that and I thought I'd get on with my work. JC

It's because I'm over-qualified. They don't want me to be in a position where I might actually have to manage staff. I don't know why, because you weren't ever really given the chance particularly. MH

Promotion of BME nurses with the necessary experience and qualifications to senior positions within the profession has therefore been slow. Previous studies have shown that though black nurses were often left in charge of wards this was not generally accompanied by promotion. Indeed, a common experience was being refused promotion in favour of white colleagues with less experience.[24] One of the midwives we spoke to had faced a similar situation when a community manager post became available with responsibility for the antenatal clinic and community midwives.

I applied for this post but did not get it ... At the time, I thought that I stood a good chance of getting the job because of my experience of having managed the antenatal clinic for fourteen months. The midwife who got the job was white, and although quite experienced, lacked the managerial experience of the antenatal clinic. RC

Some of the nurses we interviewed spoke of having to earn the respect of their white colleagues. There was also a feeling that their performance was scrutinised more than would have been the case for their white colleagues.

Some people were good, once they got used to me and they saw that I had the knowledge. JC

When I first started they'd listen to me giving advice on the phone ... I knew that if I'd said anything wrong they would have picked me up on it. [Q: And do you think that would have been, that was different to how they treated their white colleagues?] Oh yes ... but after a while, when they'd got to know me it's almost like you've passed the test. JE

Senior Management

Studies conducted in the 1980s revealed that few BME nurses made it to the top of their profession. A survey of six health authorities in 1983 found there were no black district-nursing officers, and that only two out of sixty directors of nursing services were black, as were only seven senior nurses.[25] In 1984, Louise Da-Cocodia, Manchester's first black senior nursing officer (albeit for Tameside rather than a central Manchester health authority), made the following observation:

> I recently attended a function in an adjoining area in Manchester and looked around the room to acknowledge colleagues and noticed that 75% of the District Nursing group, mainly SENs with a few SRNs were black, as were the midwives, nursing auxiliaries, the geriatric and psychiatric nurses, approximately 10% health visitors and school nurses; last but not least the child health doctor herself.[26]

Da-Cocodia went on to comment that the 'experience could be repeated in many cities in England, yet there is an under representation of blacks in the senior positions.'[27] Very little has altered in the twenty-five years since the publication of the article from which these comments were drawn. BME nurses continue to be under-represented in senior NHS posts in Britain. There are at present only two directors of nursing from BME origin in the North West, and there are currently none in Manchester.

One of the Asian doctors we spoke to expressed concerns about the lack of BME nurses in senior management positions within his NHS Trust.

> *I have been very fortunate and have done various roles, however, you very rarely see BME nurses and doctors in a high position, and that is a real problem. That is what saddens me about the NHS. In one Trust, which employs nearly 15,000 nurses and doctors and whose BME nursing staff is 14 %, they don't have even one BME nurse in their Equality and Diversity Committee because there is no BME nurse who is senior enough to be a member of the committee. This was told to me by the Nurse Director who is white!* UP

In 2003 the NHS launched its 'Breaking Through Top Talent Programme', designed to tackle racism within the service and specifically to move BME staff, including nurses, into senior positions, such as Director and Chief Executive positions through mentoring and leadership training. Few nurses originally applied. Nola Ishmael, OBE, the first black director of nursing in London and former Department of Health adviser, feels a 'lack of opportunity' stops BME nurses 'from being managerially competent and executively proficient' and accessing promotion.[28] Neslyn Watson-Druée, managing director of Beacon Organisational Development, the organisation that developed the NHS leadership, career and personal development programme which operated between 1993 and 2006, agrees. She suggests that information about career development does not always filter down to BME nurses, and that even when such information does reach them there may be some reluctance to follow a positive action programme because 'they are fearful of organisational cultures which questions why BME nurses are getting special development resources that other nurses are not.'[29]

From speaking to Nursing Directors and senior Equality and Diversity staff within the NHS in Manchester it seems that they are keenly aware of the city's shortcomings in this area. The difficulties of making BME staff aware of such schemes was referred to by one member of a Manchester Trust:

> *It was discussed at the equality and diversity groups so that the divisional directors that are there can feed it back into their teams to get representation, but it is quite difficult because we don't have a great ethnic mix within our nurses. And again in senior management, we don't have that representation.*[30]

Recruitment from BME Communities in Manchester

Since the 1980s there has been growing evidence that nursing is no longer seen as an attractive career for BME people. According to some of the comments we received, Manchester's record on recruiting students from BME communities has not been particularly strong.

> *There isn't as much recruitment of ethnic minorities within student nurses anyway. I lecture to Manchester University on equality and diversity and when I go into the lecture theatre, although there are people from different ethnic minorities in there, there aren't large numbers … as a student nurse I didn't [train with] anybody of an ethnic minority … I trained in Tameside, which is in within Greater Manchester, and … Manchester Royal [Infirmary] didn't have any [ethnic minority trainees.]*[31]

Another of our interviewees studied for a degree in Midwifery in Manchester in the early 1980s and found that she was the only black person in her group. Figures from 2006 to 2007 showed that BME communities were under-represented within the Faculty of Health and Social Care at the University of Salford, particularly in undergraduate nursing. Students, both undergraduates and postgraduates, from BME backgrounds made up just 13.6% of admissions to the Faculty, compared to 23.2% of total University admissions.[32] At the Manchester Metropolitan University, 6% of nursing students in 2000 were from ethnic minorities. (The figure was higher, 16 to 25%, on the BA (Hons) Health Studies Course, which is not a nursing qualification and is open to eighteen-year old school leavers.[33]

The negative way in which black nurses have been treated in the past is seen as the reason for the reluctance among subsequent generations to pursue nursing as a career.[34] Our interviewees supported this view.

> It's changed now because people of my age are retiring now ... we told our children not to go into nursing. They realised racism was in every part of society. JC

> We go to Africa now instead because the Caribbeans are wiser now at going into other disciplines ... the NHS is not an attractive option. CB

> In certain cultures, nursing isn't a job that you'd want your daughter to do, so people don't encourage them to move into it, and I think we've got to break down those barriers.[35]

Bureaucracy, Hierarchy and Gender

Finally, a note should be made of the wider problems relating to the hierarchies and structures of the nursing profession, the issue of gender, and the problems associated with NHS bureaucracy which have impacted on the recruitment and promotion of all nurses but seem particularly to have disadvantaged BME nurses.

During the period many of our interviewees entered British nursing, the internal hierarchies of the profession were strictly observed although relations could be easier beyond the hospitals, in community nursing.

> When I was a first year I couldn't speak to a second year because our tutor said if you're friendly ... with people you can't give them orders so then you put the patient's life ... in jeopardy. You get to second year and you can't talk to a third year nurse because of the same thing and then you get to third year and you're not allowed to mix with Staff Nurses and then by the time I got to Sister, the rules had changed; you know anybody can talk to everybody so I don't think I got much respect. JC

> You were disciplined. You weren't allowed to call your senior by their name, not to mention the Ward Sister, [or] the Matron. RC

> Everybody respected a Sister ... she had control of her ward ... [her] uniform would come back pressed and with ... paper in between ... the respect was there because everybody aspired to be a Sister ...

the Consultant ... wouldn't do a ward round unless the Sister was there. JC

It was completely different working in the community, absolutely different. Maybe it's to do with hospitals. [Q: ... It's a very different hierarchy in the community?] Flatter, isn't it? ... There's Matron, when I first started training but then became Nursing Officers, then Sisters, Senior Sisters, Sister Level 1 and RGN. It just went on and on and on, whereas in the community, as soon as you trained, you were more or less a First Level Sister so maybe that's what it was ... The nurses were different; attitudes were different. They respect people, as individuals ... I felt far more confident. I felt valued as a human being. MH

Unregulated interview processes frequently militated against equality. As the following account indicates, as late as the 1980s it was still possible to hold one-to-one interviews for nursing posts, so that the position might be given on the whim of the staff member in charge. One nurse recounted her experience in Manchester.

I'd come up for the interview and suddenly it was just like 'oh the job's gone' ... Now you have to have a proper interview process and you get a panel and everything seems quite above board. It wasn't like that in 1985, '86. You'd come up and you'd have one man or one woman who'd just sort of say 'no' almost immediately ... people say 'oh being PC ... the vetting processes and the Equal Ops employment, it's all too unfair' ... believe me, if you had to go through the system that I and probably loads of other people had to go through in order to get a job, you'd want it to be fair or to at least have a chance of being fair. One person sitting there in an office and no one knows whether you've been or not. They can say 'oh she didn't turn up', or 'put that in the bin'. No one would know. MH

Those interviewed agreed that recruitment procedures are now more robust.

I think obviously the legislation is a lot stronger so we can't go treating people the way we have in the past, so I think organisations have to be better at hiding what they do. CB

Anonymous registration and on-line application forms, for example, ensure that the information received cannot be used to discriminate from the outset. Some interviewees however believe more needs to be done to investigate what actually happens at the selection process and at interviews to ensure continued transparency and equality of opportunity. What information do the managers making the selections receive? And what assumptions and prejudices might interview panel members bring with them?

Finally, gender is another vital issue for nursing.

> *I don't think there are enough senior people that are women, let alone, black minority ethnic groups in organisations.*[36]

While nursing had traditionally been a female profession, a small but significant number of male nurses had been employed, predominantly in the psychiatric field. The immediate post-war years witnessed an influx in the number of men entering all types of nursing fields.[37] Although initially kept professionally separate, men were amalgamated onto the same nursing register as women in 1949, were accepted as members of the RCN in 1960, and under the 1975 Sex Discrimination Act the fields of midwifery and health visiting were opened up to them. In the 1960s, the new top grades of Principal Nursing Officer and Chief Nursing Officer were created and it soon became apparent that men were achieving considerable success in gaining these senior positions in nurse education and management, ahead of women. The number of men in the top grades increased eightfold between 1969 and 1972, compared to only fivefold among women.[38] This trend continued. Between the 1970s and the 1980s, the percentage of men in nursing was approximately only 10%.[39] Nonetheless, a study in 1980 found that men occupied almost half of the most senior nursing positions in management, education, and various professional organisations, trade unions, and statutory bodies.[40] Research showed that men were faster than women at achieving promotion and career progression in nursing. In 1986, one team of researchers discovered that the average time taken for men to reach nursing officer grade from qualification was 8.4 years, whilst women took on average 17.9 years (14.5 years for women with continuous careers; 22.7 years for those who took career breaks).[41] These considerable differences were attributed to the fact that male career paths, which characteristically involved long hours, home study, continuous service, and geographical mobility, were generally unobtainable for women who were more likely to take career breaks and have family responsibilities.[42] Further research shows that female nurses experience periods of career stasis when starting a family whilst male nurses often intensify their efforts to build their careers.[43] But although we know something of the individual relationships of gender and nursing, and ethnicity and nursing, we know little about the collective dynamics between gender, ethnicity and nursing, particularly the experiences of BME male nurses. The most recent report by the Royal College of

Nursing into the work-life experiences of BME nurses, for example did not include male interviewees.[44]

Summary

As an urban, multi-cultural city with huge health inequalities, Manchester was seen by our nurses as an exciting albeit challenging place to work. On the whole, the nurses we interviewed enjoyed rewarding experiences in the local health service. The biographical details below provide further confirmation that these particular nurses, midwives and health visitors carved out successful careers in spite of the barriers placed in their way. Their experiences may not be typical; many other research studies have provided less positive accounts. Nonetheless, they do confirm that:

- BME nurses in Manchester have faced difficulties at every stage of their careers, from recruitment and training, to deployment and promotion.

- Racism at both an institutional and personal level was a major cause of negative experiences in the workplace.

- BME nurses often faced racial discrimination alone. A lack of collegial support left many too embarrassed or scared to report their concerns and the fear of reprisal meant that BME nurses did not collectively challenge racism.

- Mentors offered invaluable support and advice.

- Manchester's record on the recruitment of BME nurses, and on promoting BME nurses to senior positions is generally poor.

Biographies

JASMINE EDWARDS was born in Cuba to Jamaican parents. The family eventually returned to Jamaica when she was five. She came to England in 1954 to train as a nurse at Bradford St Luke's Hospital, after applying directly to the hospital through the British Council. In 1958, after completing her State Registered Nurse qualification, Jasmine did her midwifery training in Greenwich, London, and Dartford, Kent. After qualifying as a midwife, she did her health visitor training at the Royal College of Nursing School in London. As she was sponsored by Salford she was obliged to work there for a year after qualifying. Shortly after arriving in Salford she married and started a family, taking a career break for eight and a half years. She returned to work as a Health Visitor in Stretford, and worked for eleven years between 1969 and 1980 in Old Trafford. In 1980 she went to work in Urmston, Flixton and Davyhulme. She retired at sixty. In retirement, Jasmine has done voluntary work for the Citizens Advice Bureau.

JANNETT CREESE was born in St Vincent, one of the Windward Islands, in 1940, and came to England in 1959 to undertake nurse training at St Leonard's Hospital in London. Jannett completed her State Registered Nurse certificate in 1962, receiving the Matron's Prize for proficiency throughout training, and then undertook midwifery training at Selly Oak Hospital, Birmingham, and St Mary's Hospital, Croydon. She then worked as a Staff Nurse at Mayday Hospital, Crydon. After taking time off to have children, Jannett returned as an agency nurse working at Croydon General Hospital. She combined night shifts with bringing up her growing family and was eventually promoted to a Night Sister post. In 1972 she and her family moved to Stockport, and after a brief spell at one of the local hospitals, took up a Night Sister post at Withington Hospital in Manchester where she stayed for ten years, working opposite a nursing officer and taking charge of the surgical unit. In 1982 Jannett moved to Stepping Hill Hospital in Stockport where she worked as a Night Sister on both the Care of the Elderly Unit, and the Intensive Care Unit. While working as a nurse, Jannett completed a BA Honours in Education, graduating with a 2:2 degree. Jannett retired from nursing in 1995 due to ill health, after thirty-six years in the profession. Since then she has, amongst other things, been a tutor for the College of Nursing, learnt sign language and supported deaf students in Stockport College and

Bolton University, trained First Aid at Work students at the local college, worked for Victim Support in Stockport for fifteen years, and performed voluntary work with local BME groups, the Police Independent Advisory Group, and her local Methodist Church. In 2009 she started a group for over-sixties black people in Stockport. In 2008 Jannett was voted Stockport's Volunteer of the Year in the 'My Place' Citizens Awards. Her autobiography, *My Windward Side*, was published in 2002 by Stockport Metropolitan Borough Council Library and Information Service.

REMI CLARKE was born in Nigeria and came to England when she was eighteen to study nursing. After completing her A' Levels, Remi began her three-years general nurse training in 1968 at Hertford County Hospital, and went straight on to do her midwifery training at Rush Green Hospital, Romford in Essex, and at North Hertfordshire Hospital, Hitchin in Hertfordshire. In August 1972 she was appointed Staff Midwife at St. Albans City Hospital, and was promoted to Midwifery Sister a year later. In May 1975, Remi took time out to do a course in Special and Intensive Nursing Care of the Newborn at the Jessop Hospital for Children in Sheffield. After completing the course she helped to upgrade and ensure the smooth running of the Special Care Baby Unit at Hemel Hempstead Hospital before returning to St Albans as a Senior Midwifery Sister. In July 1983, she left to work in Nigeria for a year, as a Nurse/Midwifery Sister. Remi returned to Britain in 1984. In March 1985, following a brief four-month stint at Stepping Hill Hospital, Stockport, she was appointed as a Staff Midwife at Withington Hospital postnatal ward. A month later she was promoted to Midwifery Sister, taking charge of the antenatal clinic for nearly two years. In December 1986 she took up the post of Community Midwifery Sister in South Manchester, and in 1995/1996 was appointed Midwifery Team Leader. In the same year she took her DPSM/BSC in Midwifery Practice. Remy retired in 2006 after thirty-eight years in the NHS, twenty-one of them spent with South Manchester Hospital Trust. In retirement, Remi continues to do the odd bank shift mainly in the antenatal/community clinics for South Manchester University Hospitals.

CAROL BAXTER, CBE is a health care policy developer, and is Head of Equality and Diversity and Human Rights at NHS Employers. Carol was born in Jamaica in 1950. She came to England in 1971 to do her nurse, midwifery and health visitor training in Salford. She then combined a career break to bring up her family with a Masters degree in Community Medicine in

1978, and later a Doctorate, at the University of Manchester, and went on to work as a health promotion officer with Manchester Health Authority. In 1995 she took up posts as a Senior Lecturer at the Universities of Central Lancashire and Manchester, and later became Professor of Nursing at Middlesex University. In 2002 she was seconded for three years to join the equality and diversity team at the Department of Health's Human Resources Directorate, where she managed a project supporting improved access for black and ethnic minority people into the nursing and midwifery professions. She was appointed to her current position at NHS Employers in 2005. Carol was a founder member and Chair of MACHEM (Manchester Action Committee for Healthcare for Ethnic Minorities). She is also the author of the seminal texts – *The Black Nurse: An Endangered Species* (published by Training in Health and Race in 1988), and *Managing Diversity and Inequality in Health Care* (published by Baillière Tindall and the Royal College of Nursing in 2001). She was awarded a CBE in 2009.

NEISHA FIELDER was born in Guyana in 1947. She came to England at the age of eighteen. She trained as a State Registered Nurse at St Charles hospital, Ladbroke Grove, London, and later went on to complete her midwifery training at Edgeware Hospital, London. Afterwards she took a career break to have children, and she and her family moved from London to Stockport. She was employed on night duty, part-time for about a year on the kidney unit at Withington Hospital, and then as a school nurse at Reddish Valley School for a year. She then did her health visitor training sponsored by Stockport Health Authority. Neisha worked as a Lecturer at Stockport College for seven years before resuming her health-visiting career in 2001. She has an Open University Degree and an Adult Further Education Teachers' Certificate. She is currently a Health Visitor for Manchester PCT, based at Longsight Health Centre. Neisha is also a Magistrate and is involved in the Union, as Chair of the Equalities Committee of the National Professional Committee which is the elected body representing the twelve Unite regions and respective community nurse specialisms.

MICHELLE HALLER was born in Paddington, London, of Jamaican parentage. She began her Registered General Nurse training at Northwick Park Hospital, Kenton Middlesex in 1981. After qualifying she did agency nursing in London Hospitals, and worked for over a year on the cardiac ward of Northwick Park Hospital. In 1985 she took up a nursing post on the gastrointestinal ward at Manchester Royal Infirmary. In 1987 she applied for and was accepted on to the training for Registered Nurse Mental Handicap with South Manchester Health Authority. She has since then worked on the resettlement of people with learning disabilities from long stay hospitals such as Calderstones and Brockhall; as a care manager for people with learning disabilities based in West Didsbury; and as a Health of the Nation Care Nurse for Tameside Health Authority promoting effective health care for people with learning disabilities. Michelle currently works as an Inspector for the Care Quality Commission inspecting the full range of registered adult care services.

Finally, we could not end this section without also including biographical notes for Louise Da-Cocodia.

LOUISE DA-COCODIA, Manchester's first senior black nursing officer sadly died in 2008 and was not interviewed for this book. She came to Britain in 1955 from Jamaica to train as a nurse at St. Olive's Hospital in London, a post she obtained through a direct application made from Jamaica. She later moved to Manchester where she spent the rest of her life. Louise enjoyed a twenty-six-year career in nursing, ending as a Senior Nursing Manager. She was actively involved in the local community and race relations. She was involved with the Arawak Walton Housing Association, which helps develop sustainable multi-cultural neighbourhoods, had acted as a consultant and advisor on the Moss Side and Hulme Task Force, was deputy chair of Voluntary Action Manchester, and chair of Moss Side and Hulme Women's Action Forum. She also played a key role in setting up Cariocca Enterprises, which was formed to develop business programmes and projects for the benefit of inner-city Manchester residents. She was a member of the Hytner Tribunal set up to look into the causes of the Moss Side riots in the early 1980s, and an active member of the Council's race sub-committee. In 1992 she was awarded the British Empire Medal and, in 1995, was one of the first recipients of the Manchester Race Awards, launched by the Council and Manchester Council for Community Relations. She served for fouteen years as a Justice of the Peace on the Manchester Bench, and was a non-executive member of Manchester Health Authority. She was a former Deputy Lord Lieutenant of Manchester, and received an MBE in 2005.[45]

5

Doctors

From the late 1950s onwards, imbalances in the supply and demand of doctors, intensified by the emigration of UK-trained doctors, created shortages in Britain which were resolved through mass recruitment from the Indian sub-continent. The professional structures of medicine had been reinforced by the creation of the NHS: divisions between hospital consultants and GPs had sharpened and GPs were generally perceived to be of lower status, although highly popular with the public. The landscape of medical practice was shaped by hierarchies of specialties, training institutions and geographical locations. In general practice, single-handed practices in deprived urban areas and remote rural locations remained unpopular. In hospital medicine, specialties like mental health and care of the elderly were undersubscribed, largely because of their historical lower status and power. Teaching hospitals had long been the pinnacle of medical training. In the 1950s, the expansion of postgraduate training through the appointment of postgraduate Deans based in medical schools, responsible for establishing courses and linking central and peripheral hospitals, was widely welcomed.[1] Nevertheless, it perpetuated hierarchical patterns across regions and reinforced the dominance of teaching hospitals like the MRI. Regions also tended to favour local medical students and professional networks and established connections helped to secure prestigious jobs. Overseas doctors entering Britain during this period found that career opportunities were contingent on these broader hierarchies. We shall see below how our interviewees experienced many difficulties in achieving their desired training and career posts and yet remained committed to medical practice.

BME Doctors and Racism

Prior to the 1980s much of the debate on overseas doctors focused on their professional competence, and was devoted to the issue of registration. The Merrison Report (1975) criticised the level of skill and care among overseas doctors. Following its recommendations, most overseas doctors applying for temporary registration in Britain were required to pass an examination which tested their English skills and medical knowledge (TRAB test; later renamed PLAB, Professional and Linguistic Assessment Board). Very little interest was shown in the postgraduate training and promotion prospects of overseas doctors in the NHS.

A study by the Community Relations Commission in 1976 was the first to raise concerns over the career progression of overseas doctors when it suggested: 'There is evidence that overseas doctors are not progressing equally to their British trained colleagues once they are working in United Kingdom Hospitals.'[2] In the same year as this report was published, the Overseas Doctors Association (ODA) was established to 'protect and promote the interests of overseas doctors in the UK'. The ODA, whose headquarters were in Manchester, dismissed the accusation that overseas doctors were ill-qualified and ill-trained as unfair. Rather, they claimed that overseas doctors arrived with no experience of the British medical system and little professional support, which meant they were unable to find suitable jobs, and ended up working in areas for which they had not specialised. This situation led to a lot of dissatisfaction among overseas doctors.

Leading on from these early concerns, the first major studies of overseas doctors were published in the 1980s, often in close collaboration with the ODA. Work by David J. Smith for the Policy Studies Institute (1980), and Muhammad Anwar and Ameer Ali for the Committee for Racial Equality (1987), drew attention to the racial disadvantage and discrimination faced by overseas doctors in the NHS, and showed how overseas doctors, who were mostly from ethnic minorities, faced significant barriers in training, deployment, and career development.[3] Smith and Anwar and Ali also showed that the assumption that language barriers prevented the progress of overseas doctors, as implied by the Merrison recommendations, was unfounded. Instead, their investigations revealed that it was specific processes within the medical profession, including institutional and personal racism, which served to obstruct the career paths of overseas doctors. The authors made several recommendations to prevent exploitation and to promote equality of opportunity for BME doctors, including the introduction of planned training programmes, more transparent selection and recruitment practices, and ethnic monitoring.[4]

Since the publication of these studies, further research has been carried out which has shown the continuing presence of racism in medicine. In more recent years the focus has shifted to look at the differential experiences of BME doctors practising in particular specialisms (e.g. general practice, geriatrics), on racial discrimination in medical schools, and on the contrasting experiences of overseas-trained and British-trained BME doctors.[5]

Joining the NHS

Surveys have shown that most overseas doctors came to Britain to obtain further qualifications, specialist training and experience.[6] Our overseas interviewees were no different:

> I was ambitious. I went to learn medicine. I wanted to get to the top of medical school in England. I wanted to get my MRCP, which was very highly thought of, and which I obtained. SC

> I faced discrimination in India, which was my own country. I was trained in India and did my diploma in child health in India. I got a distinction but I was not given the opportunity to do my post-graduation MD. In India, you have to be selected to do your post-graduation. I was discriminated against because of my caste – sadly this is common in India. I was first to be interviewed out of 1,500 applicants because of my merit but I was then told that I was not successful because I did not belong to a certain caste and hence I left India and came to the UK in 1982 to pursue my career here. UP

> I think my whole aim was to widen my horizons and look at how medicine is practised in the developed world in comparison to the underdeveloped world. KC

> I graduated in '87. I think that was a very important juncture in my career. I spoke to my Professor of Community Medicine and she said Johns Hopkins but I always liked the British health care and medical education system, maybe because of my liking of the NHS. There was the same health care system in Pakistan and that was a little bit of commonality plus I got motivated by a number of people who were doing public health and playing a leadership role to improve health system outcomes. MA

Familiarity with the medical system in Britain, and preparedness for securing education and training differed among our interviewees.

> When I came here I had absolutely no idea. I didn't know what PLAB meant and what exam I had to finish before working in the UK. I had two of my friends who had come one year earlier and I stayed with them. They helped me, supported me and guided me. UP

I think the interesting thing is the Commonwealth countries; they have many similarities to the British system so you can find your way round, but if you're coming from a very different country, like for example, if you're coming from Poland, probably it would be too difficult. Now, I understand those people because their problems are similar to ours, rather than to those coming from India and Pakistan. PT

The day I got out of medical school my ticket was ready. He [his father] said 'here's your ticket, go and spend three months on holiday in England, meet with the right people in your intended career path'. I had a very good head start. Now the advice I give to other people who come to me for guidance is do your homework, invest your time on exploring and choosing the right career path before you embark on your career journey, otherwise these highly ambitious professionals may waste their resources and time unduly. MA

I wanted to apply for a public health SHO [Senior House Officer] job. I was told I have to start from SHO, as in clinical medicine. I emailed people and so on and then I realised the training starts with Special Registrar level. I didn't know that SHO jobs are very rare. It's not part of the training. PT

Much of the concern with overseas doctors in the 1970s concerned communication, language and culture, which culminated in the introduction of the PLAB test. Perceived 'language problems' were used to justify the exam failure and lack of career progression of overseas doctors. They also fuelled claims that overseas doctors provided a poor standard of patient care.[7] Smith, on the contrary, found that about two-thirds of overseas-qualified doctors had no significant language handicap when assessed using an objective test he had devised.[8] He also found, unsurprisingly, that the language skills of overseas doctors improved the longer they had been in the UK.[9] Our interviewees addressed the cultural difficulties they had faced when coming to the UK and beginning work in the NHS. They focused not so much on language but on other forms of communication and institutional cultures.

Our culture is different. In India we don't use the words like 'please' and 'thank you' in our day-to-day language. They are formal words, which we use only when we write letters. In 1982, I was told by a senior nurse that I was rude, and I was shocked! I was very upset, but I knew her well so I asked her, 'why did you say that' and she told me you don't use words like 'please' and 'thank you'. That day I learnt one of the best lessons of my life, I changed my communication style, I started using 'please' and 'thank you' and over the years, the way I speak to my colleagues, my patients and my team and anyone

I meet has changed. Now I provide training to many overseas doctors on communication skills and Britishness. I tell my juniors that it is not what you think of yourself that is important but what others think of you. UP

There are a lot of things about communication, including verbal communication, body language, presentation skills and all other things which are part of the ways you link with other people, irrespective of whether they are your PA, patients, peers or your boss or whatever. So I think these are becoming very, very important skills for success in professional life. Basically, I'm talking about emotional intelligence; the softer skills one needs to learn and develop over the years. MA

I was shocked really when I first started … When I say I was shocked, I'm not saying that was a negative experience but with my background and culture and everything, I felt like I'm in another world. Everyone talks differently. I don't mean the language. It was the jargon and especially in public health, maybe it's a total difference underpinning things and so on. PT

Over half of the overseas doctors we interviewed came to Britain around the time that immigration and registration controls were being tightened. Overseas doctors who came to Britain from the late 1970s onwards have struggled with immigration controls and visas.

It's not that easy. It's a matter of getting a visa and then you have to apply and then you need permission from the university and you have to show the finances. Plenty of things go on, and it's a very, very, big step, a big decision in your life if you're coming down here … when you are a student you are not supposed to do any other work here. You are allowed to some extent but you're only spending money so you must be from a good family background with money and resources and finances. SA

There have also been significant issues with registration. Following the Merrison Report (1975), the General Medical Council (GMC) withdrew recognition of medical qualifications for full registration from all Indian colleges because it was not satisfied as to the standard of these qualifications. (Recognition had already been withdrawn from Pakistani doctors in 1972 after that country left the Commonwealth, and from Sri Lanka in the same year.) The withdrawal of recognition provoked a widespread revoke of reciprocity within the Commonwealth, which inevitably caused problems for those returning to their countries of origin. In Britain, a two-tier system of 'full' and 'limited' registration evolved. 'Temporary Registration' status was given to overseas doctors, followed by assessment of their medical and linguistic abilities through the PLAB test. Changes to the immigration laws in 1985 meant that overseas doctors no longer had unrestricted right of entry and employment in Britain. Instead work-permits were granted to those holding career posts. Those seeking post-graduate training were granted a permit-free period of up to four years, which was extended to six years in 1997.

Upon their arrival, most overseas doctors have little or no intention of permanently settling down in Britain. Studies conducted in the 1980s estimated that between 82 and 85% of overseas doctors intended to return to their countries of origin.[10] Only about one-third of these overseas doctors, however, achieved their ambitions of obtaining further training in Britain and of returning to the Indian sub-continent.[11] The doctors who remained in Britain did so for a number of reasons. Some did not achieve their career goals, while others stayed for personal reasons (e.g. marriage; family commitments; simply liked it in England). Some of the doctors we interviewed had expected to return upon completion of their training but had instead remained in Britain, mainly for personal reasons.

> *When an overseas doctor comes to the UK, in the first three years he/she always wants to go back. However, after five to six years of staying in Britain, there is a gradual change that takes place and you don't want to go back. That is what happened to me. I always tell my juniors that if you want to go back, go back within four years and if you don't then after six years of your stay in Britain, it is difficult to go back.* UP

> *I had no intention of settling here but then circumstances take over and here I am after thirty-two years.* KC

> *I kept coming and going, keeping them [his family] happy and helping them … And then the problem starts; not the problem, but the change of mind starts.* SA

Training and Working in the NHS

Research has shown that overseas doctors also found it difficult to put together their training programme and then to pursue it.[12] Many of our overseas respondents had difficulty in securing their first training posts in the NHS. They often had to make more applications for subsequent posts than their white British colleagues, and had to find 'unplanned training' via honorary, part-time and locum posts, which were not recognised as specialist training.

I passed my exam and I got junior jobs, not so easily, but with difficulty. [Q: Was there a lot of competition for these jobs?] Tremendous competition and tremendous indirect discrimination ... They looked at your face and that was all that they needed to do about your employment and there was nothing you could do about it. SC

I passed my PLAB in 1982 and started applying for jobs. I think I had to apply to seventy jobs but was not shortlisted even for one job. Then I met a true English gentleman, Dr Welch, who really helped me and offered me a clinical attachment, offered me locum jobs. UP

It's not that easy to get a job here ... That was the most difficult part ... I started getting unpaid jobs because straight away nobody gives you a paid job because they don't know about your experience, how you're treating the patient, are you qualified or not ... You start doing applications, improving your English ... applying for the different jobs. The first job is always difficult. SA

You used to apply, apply, apply. Nobody wanted to even send you an interview. Nobody wanted to even know you. You'd gone and knocked at so many doors, met so many people, but it was very difficult and for almost eighteen months to two years, I thought I was exploited as well. People took me on and if normally the job was going for twenty-five thousand, so they said 'fine, if you want to accept it, we're going to give you ten thousand'. So you had no choice when you have a family, two kids and no home. KC

BME doctors graduating from British medical schools could also face difficulties in applying for and competing for their first posts after qualifying. As Aneez Esmail explained:

It was very straightforward getting jobs if you were a house doctor because the university had a responsibility to find you a job ... But I remember when I applied for my first job after university ... I was applying for many more jobs compared to white colleagues ... for every one job they had to apply for I had to apply for ten to fifteen. AE

Discrimination clearly begins at the process of shortlisting and selection, as one doctor stated:

You go and sit in the selection committee and you can find out that your chances are going down and down with no apparent reason why it should be so ... Election and interview is one of the best ways of doing it whereas selection always tends to discriminate ... selection committee may be whatever it is but is always a discriminatory role. SC

Groundbreaking research by Aneez Esmail and Sam Everington published in the *BMJ* in 1993, in which matched pairs of CVs from false Asian and English applicants were submitted for forty-six job applications for twenty-three hospital posts, showed that names alone were enough to determine the frequency of an applicant's success or failure in being shortlisted.[13] Their enquiries found that applicants with English-sounding names were twice as likely to be selected for interview. When they repeated this study in 1997 a lower proportion of Asian than English candidates were again shortlisted (36% versus 52%). Aneez and Everington argue that consultants are to blame for the discrimination as it is they who are responsible for shortlisting for junior posts.[14]

Some of the doctors we interviewed talked about how they handled these situations, adapting their own approach and behaviour to accommodate the discrepancies and inadequacies of the larger system.

> *When I was a junior doctor I learned my own way to deal with it, so whenever a job came up and I really wanted, it, I'd actually make a point of going to see the people out there, and it wasn't sort of the done thing, but I said well I must go and make some excuse, like I've come to the consultant, find out what it's like, and the whole idea was that they could see me, and place me in a different setting, rather than just as an overseas student doctor … I made the extra effort to present myself where I would be looked at differently, rather than just as a foreign name.* AE

> *And then you have to face a very competitive environment for your career progression, which is basically you are competing on open ground with all the local graduates. I never ever shied away from that and plus I did not moan about any unfairness or blame the system. God willing, most of the time I was successful in my pursuits, irrespective of the competition. I never looked at things that being overseas I was so called disadvantaged in that process but no doubt I had to go an extra mile to achieve those successes. If unsuccessful, I evaluated the situation, thinking about what I should have done better. I am sure that attitude helped me to grow out of crisis rather leaving a negative impact on me. I did my best to take the positive out of such situations and it paid off over the years.* MA

All the overseas doctors we spoke to referred to the importance of mentors who had guided their initial entry on to the NHS career ladder.

> *I had a good entrance to Birmingham University Medical School where somehow I was favoured by the Professor, and I got myself established as a trainee there with luck, and I met a lot of very nice people who helped me tremendously.* SC

I was fortunate to meet a lot of wonderful people in all walks of life and progressed very well in the NHS. I have been very fortunate and have done various roles. I would like to thank the many wonderful people whom I have met during the course of my work in the NHS. Many people have supported me, guided me, helped me and listened to my concerns. UP

This gentleman, a very nice surgeon, he helped me and he acted as one of my referees ... he agreed [to be his referee] after having a discussion with me and seeing that I was very much interested and very punctual and attending and very much personally involved with the patient. SA

Any deficiencies which I had since my graduation, I did my best to work hard with advice from my colleagues and mentors to learn and fill such gaps. MA

I think I was very fortunate and very lucky that right from the word go the very consultant I had in my clinical attachment was a very wise person. He knew exactly what the world is like and what's expected and how you could move forward. KC

Nevertheless, inability to obtain the appropriate type and amount of training due to institutional discrimination can make it difficult for overseas doctors to pursue the specialties they desire, forcing them to modify their career choices and enter less popular specialties.

Unpopular Specialisms

Overseas doctors are disproportionately employed in the least popular specialties, including geriatrics and psychiatry. These specialties have traditionally been unpopular among British graduates, and have therefore offered faster career progression for overseas doctors unable to pursue their first choice specialty. Meagre resources, high workload, and poor working conditions made these disciplines particularly unattractive. In 1981, for example, almost 84% of registrars in geriatrics, and 59% of registrars in mental illness, were from overseas. At consultant level, 43.4% of consultants in geriatrics and 24.3% of consultants in mental illness were from overseas, as opposed to 16.2% in anaesthetics and 8.6% in general surgery.[15] Accident and emergency is another low status specialty that suffers from recruitment problems due to the excessive workload and the patients it attracts, particularly within large inner-city casualty departments.[16] Between 1983 and 1985, 35% of consultants in accident and emergency were born overseas. By the end of the twentieth century, the proportion of non-white consultants remained highest in geriatrics (30.4%), accident and emergency (27%) and general psychiatry (24%). Their numbers were lowest in general surgery (14.1%).[17]

Outside the hospitals, general practice was another area where many migrant Asian doctors found jobs, especially in single-handed practices in deprived urban areas, or remote rural locations.[18] Over the last sixty years the proportion of single-handed GPs has decreased considerable. In 1948, around 50% of GPs were in single-handed practices, many of them in deprived urban areas; in 2008, fewer than 10% of GPs worked in single-handed practices although these were still concentrated in deprived urban areas, or remote rural locations.[19] Since the 1950s, single-handed GPs have tended to be overseas-trained and of BME origin.[20]

Some of our interviewees experienced difficulties in finding jobs and securing promotion in the specialties of their choice. While some persevered and eventually succeeded, others abandoned their original choices and moved on. Their comments reveal how joining unpopular specialties might guarantee a better chance of promotion to higher grades.

> *My colleagues said Umesh go into psychiatry you'll get job tomorrow. I said no, either I do paediatrics or I go back.* UP

> *My consultant was a very nice gentleman and I'm sure he was worldly-wise and he knew what people coming from ethnic background wanted to pursue and he was very honest with me. He said 'Kailash, if you want to pursue your hospital career in paediatrics' – in those days paediatrics was a sought after speciality – 'you'll have to struggle' … and he actually advised me that 'if you want to pursue a hospital career then you look into specialties like psychiatry or geriatrics' or something … Less popular, less romantic and less sought after by Caucasians, let's put it that way.* KC

The locum work he was offered in paediatrics meant that getting an extension of his visa was '*a real struggle*'. In the end he found a job in accident and emergency at Ancoats Hospital in Manchester, and later pursued training in general practice. Another doctor we interviewed came to Britain with the intention of pursuing a career in orthopaedic surgery.

> *But to do so here you need to do the general surgery fellowship first. My home country experience in surgery was very limited, so I decided to try radiology.* SA

Geographical Hierarchies

Research has shown that geography is also 'decisive' in shaping the career progression, specialty choice, and job satisfaction of overseas doctors.[21] As Bornat et al. confirmed in their interviews with South Asian geriatricians: local hierarchies had 'a commitment to employing people who studied in the region' and 'overseas doctors had to fit themselves into what was already an uneven mosaic of opportunity.'[22] This opinion was shared by some of our interviewees.

The NHS generally favours local graduates and stops overseas doctors climbing on the seniority ladder. SA

And then you have to go openly in a very competitive environment, which is basically you are competing on open ground with all the local graduates. MA

BME doctors often found themselves based in general hospitals in less attractive geographical areas, rather than in the larger and more prestigious teaching hospitals that offered greater experience and training in a variety of specialisms.[23] In 1960, a report by the Consultant Services Committee stated that many hospitals outside the teaching centre in Manchester were almost entirely dependent on overseas doctors for resident and non-resident junior medical staff.[24] This pattern was repeated across the country. By the 1980s, the prevalence of BME doctors to practice on the geographical and institutional margins appears to have even been the same for British trained BME medical graduates.

I always noted that it was interesting that none of the Asian students – there were no Afro-Caribbeans at that time – none of the Asian students ever got the jobs in the teaching hospitals. We always ended up on the periphery ... I also learned not to apply for certain jobs. There's no point applying for a teaching hospital job because they were going to be given to their blue-eyed boys ... so I learned to apply in places where there was a better chance. AE

Lack of access to postgraduate teaching in specialties of their choice meant that many overseas doctors found it difficult to complete postgraduate qualifications.

In paediatrics, the only option I had was to do locum work ... even getting extension of visa was a real struggle for me so after a tiny bit of applying here, there and everywhere, not getting anywhere, I ended up doing a job in A&E. KC

As a consequence, they often found like the interviewee here that the only choice available to them was general practice, usually in an undesirable location.

Discipline and Conduct

A disproportionate number of BME clinicians are suspended and referred to the GMC each year. BME doctors are six times more likely to appear before the Professional Conduct Committee of the GMC than their white counterparts. In their research on the assessment and appraisal of clinicians, Abel and Esmail have shown how institutional racism is an important factor in the assessment of physicians when their performance raises concern.[25] One of our interviewees, an adviser to the second stage complaints for the Healthcare Commission, talks about the inherent bias in the disciplinary system.

> *I've got at least seven or eight doctors who have been suspended who shouldn't have been suspended, and I doubt whether the system would have suspended them if they were white doctors. Patient safety and their well being should be at the heart of our duty as doctors but it is equally important to make sure that all doctors are treated fairly and equally and action taken is proportionate. Most doctors need help, support, guidance and mentoring and not punishment. When rarely there are doctors whose performance is so bad that it puts patients' lives at risk or whose conduct or behaviour brings our profession into disrepute, we should get rid of them. This is important to protect our patients and for the sake of professional reputation.* UP

BME single-handed GPs seem particularly vulnerable to discrimination on account of their specialty and ethnicity. An analysis of the GMC's fitness to practice hearings in 2008–2009 showed that single handed GPs of *all* ethnic backgrounds were six times as likely to appear before the GMC as GPs in group practices.[26] Coupled with the wider evidence on the over representation of BME doctors in disciplinary proceedings, this suggests that particular attention should be paid to the experiences of BME single-handed GPs.

Overseas versus British Trained and Qualified

It is clear from listening to the life stories of the BME doctors that experiences could differ according to whether one was British or overseas-qualified. Even in our small sample, BME doctors graduating from British medical schools were more likely to progress in their chosen specialty, and to report less direct experience of discrimination. In the 1980s it was usual to find all ethnic minority doctors treated as a homogenous group. More recently there has been a shift in distinguishing between BME doctors born, trained and qualified in Britain from those born, trained and qualified overseas. One doctor commented on his own personal experience of this change.

> *I had a foreign name and so I was an overseas doctor and therefore faced everything that came with that … it's much more subtle now because they now distinguish between British-qualified doctors and overseas-qualified doctors, so in a way people can say well you're alright, because you're now in that block.* AE

> *Britain is a very fair country and most people I have met have been just wonderful. However, sadly there is discrimination and differential treatment and some Trusts do tend to treat overseas-trained doctors much more harshly. We need a system where we can identify poor performance early so that these doctors can be helped, supported and guided. This would help us to protect patients and also to support doctors.* UP

Relations with Patients and Colleagues: Day-to-Day Racism

Personal experiences of overt racial discrimination were spoken of as rare among those we interviewed, although some acknowledged that attacks did occasionally occur.

> *I never experienced any discrimination or racism. My patients were very good and the nurses were fantastic.* UP

> *Never, never had a whisper of it, either from patients or from staff. I could never remember even being conscious of it … certainly in my student years I would have thought, I think everybody was aware of it and they'd sometimes comment on it, but only as a matter of interest, not otherwise.* NM

> *If you are in A&E, as a casualty officer, they have to see you whether they like it or don't like it. But when you come to general practice … that's the first time it really impacted on me … There used to be occasions that yes even bluntly patients, occasionally, very occasionally, used to say 'I don't want to see this Asian Doctor' or whatever. 'Why can't I see my own?'* KC

When specific incidences of discrimination on grounds of race were recalled they were usually distanced from their own personal experiences. One doctor, for example, recalled an incident at the MRI when the appointment of another BME consultant, caused 'some rumblings in the hospital'. He compared the MRI to Leeds General Infirmary, which was apparently renowned for its conservatism and closed ranks.

> That was a very conservative hospital, very conservative, very much on the lines of the London teaching hospital ... they were a very closed society there in terms of their consultant numbers, and they took a relatively selected group of people ... MRI had that flavour, but as I say I think it had it to a much lesser extent and a more pragmatic lesser extent and I think it reflected the community around it you know it sort of had one foot in both camps, the Manchester pragmatism and the national conservatism really. NM

All the doctors we spoke to acknowledged that racism was inherent to the way in which the NHS was run but that it was possible to find ways of working with the system and to challenge it.

> [Q: Did you feel that the health authority and the local authority were interested in issues around race?] They were not interested and discrimination was quite rampant. In some cases this was justified, if you justify that the jobs in British hospitals are meant for British people. On the other hand, discrimination is not justified if you think jobs should be for the best people. If a doctor was practicing medicine in England, be he Chinese or Indian or from Timbuktu, if he has the qualifications and knowledge he should be treated [the same]. But at that time, I'm afraid even now, this is not so ... discrimination is like sex, it doesn't happen in our society, does it? SC

> There is 'institutional racism' in public services. 'Islamophobia' at that time was not that big a social issue ... Being a Pakistani Muslim with a beard, I frequently noticed a feeling of dislike and intolerance towards my appearance. Disheartened fellows either go back or try their luck outside the NHS. I decided to fight on. SA

> If we didn't get anywhere, blame the system, or blame that or this, all because of racism, because of my colour and yes, there are in situations racism, here and there. We all know about that. But don't give up. Fight. KC

Nor are professional bodies immune from discriminatory practices. 43% of the membership of the British Medical Association is from BME groups, but when it comes to the national committees that number reduces to less than 15%. Our interviewees highlighted their experiences of these organisations.

I'm on the national BMA Council. But there ... whatever people say, it's a lip service. If you are a BME you have to struggle in even those organisations, and in Trade Unions as well ... for example, BMA Council is made up of thirty-two people, I was the only Asian. I was the only Asian on so big a Council ... Same exact thing happened in GMC ... if the BMA wants to survive, they have to really look into and encourage people from ethnic minorities to give leadership. KC

The GMC it became clear had no mechanism of monitoring or anything, and we forced them to look at the whole process. Why was it that Asians were twelve times more likely to be brought before the GMC? What was going on here? And you could see it was untenable for them to continue. And actually it started a root and branch reform of the GMC. AE

As the biographies at the end of this chapter indicate, many of the doctors we spoke to have in various ways sought to raise the profile of the issues affecting BME doctors and this development of a collective BME voice has been helpful in focusing the profession's attention on the difficulties.

Career Development and Promotion

Research in the 1980s showed that overseas doctors waited longer to achieve promotion to higher grades and that many struggled to reach consultant level. BME doctors (whether British/EEA/or overseas qualified) are currently under-represented in the consultant grades and over-represented at registrar and senior house officer levels within the hospital system in Britain. In 2003, only 17% of South Asian doctors were consultants compared with 42% of white doctors.[27]

A report in 1968 stated that of the 300 doctors from India and Pakistan practising in Manchester, only one was a consultant.[28] While the situation has improved it would seem that BME doctors are still underrepresented at consultant level. Table 5.1 shows the current percentage of consultants by ethnicity for the Central Manchester and Manchester Children's Hospitals NHS Foundation Trust. In comparison, 50.3% of consultants (all specialties) at the Pennine Acute NHS Trust are from BME groups.

Even when BME doctors reach consultant level discrimination against them persists. This is most notable in the handing out of distinction awards. These awards were introduced at the formation of the NHS in 1948 and were designed to persuade the most senior and influential members of the medical profession to accept the new hospital system. Designed to award merit and supposedly linked to performance appraisal, distinction awards (or Clinical Excellence Awards as they have been known since 2003/2004) have been the source of widespread criticism for the way in which a secret and unfair allocation process tends to privilege certain specialties, and discriminates against non-white, as well as women consultants. Despite reform to the performance pay system inequalities persist.[29] In 2003, Esmail and Everington showed that 56% of white consultants had been awarded discretionary points, whilst 41% of non-white consultants had been given such awards.[30]

Table 5.1: Ethnicity of consultants, Central Manchester and Manchester Children's Hospitals NHS Foundation Trust

Ethnic Origin	Consultants (all specialties)
White	70.7%
Mixed	1.1%
Asian	19.1%
Black	3.2%
Chinese	2.7%
Any other ethnic group	1.7%
Not Stated	2.0%

Source: Data provided by NHS Trusts under Freedom of Information.

BME Doctors in Senior Management

There is also an under-representation of BME doctors in senior management roles. Racism was again viewed by some of our interviewees as a key factor.

The NHS must have more BME leaders in Board and senior management positions. But we must appoint the right people to do the right job. UP

There's still a problem and where the challenge is now is if you look in who holds power in the NHS, the Medical Directors, the Chief Executives, so really the challenge now is to change that. AE

I have always said that for any society both positive and negative discrimination is wrong. But positive action by encouraging, providing training and the necessary leadership skills to their BME nurses and doctors is not wrong. If we don't do it, then the system won't change. UP

BME Entry to British Medical Schools

The demography of medical schools has changed considerably since the 1960s when the majority of students were white, male, middle class school leavers.[31] By 2003, over 60% of entrants were female and over 30% of all students came from BME backgrounds. However the majority of students were still predominantly from professional and managerial backgrounds. Since 1999, numbers of medical students have increased by around 25% as a result of a joint initiative by the Department of Health and the Higher Education Funding Council for England to tackle the national shortage of doctors through the creation of four new medical schools and expansion of graduate entry programmes, as well as increasing the overall number of places. The ratio of applicants to places currently stands at 8:1 although this has decreased since the 1970s. Applications from ethnic minorities increased from 11% in 1981 to 30% in 2003 and to 36% in 2008; and two-thirds of BME students came from Asian backgrounds.[32] Longitudinal analysis of changing patterns is limited as data on the ethnicity of medical and dental students only began to be collected in 1989; before this time estimates were made on the basis of indexing non-European surnames.

Students from minority ethnic backgrounds are now over-represented in medical schools, as indeed they are in dental and pharmacy schools, although application and acceptance rates differ between ethnic groups. Recent data suggests that some second-generation ethnic groups now have the same chances of success as their white counterparts. White British and Asian British applicants share the best chance of success in gaining a place at medical school: 73% of applicants from these groups are offered a place compared to 65% of Irish and 45% of black Caribbean British applicants.[33] The differential acceptance rate for ethnic groups suggests that some ethnic groups may be experiencing discrimination during the selection procedure. As we have seen through the experiences of our BME clinicians, securing a job is highly contingent on the specifics of the recruitment process.

> *You know there was a time when Manchester never interviewed medical students and it had the fairest admissions policy of all, and now they're interviewing and there are major differences. And I've seen this happen in other places; it's a sort of retrenching.* AE

But analysis is further complicated by the additional factors of gender and class. In all ethnic groups, female applicants have a higher acceptance rate and there are significant inter-ethnic differences in social background and educational attainment. Research into the social background of students applying to medical schools in 1994/1995 and 1996/1997 showed that white, black, and Indian medical school applicants shared a similar socio-economic profile whilst applicants from Bangladeshi, Chinese, and Pakistani communities tended to have a lower social class background.[34] Indian students have a higher chance of getting good GCSE results than students from other ethnic groups and these are used as the main indicator of academic potential.[35] Efforts have been made to identify how individuals from disadvantaged and minority ethnic backgrounds can be encouraged to apply for medical schools.[36] But the most recent evidence from 2008 shows that the majority of medical students come from the higher social classes; only 4% of students come from semi-skilled and unskilled occupational backgrounds.[37] It may be that class, rather than ethnicity, is the barrier disadvantaging some BME applicants to medicine.

Gender

Like ethnicity, gender has long been problematic in medicine and BME female doctors have been subject to discrimination on both counts. The rise of women in medicine from the post-war years to the 2000s is the most notable demographic shift of the period. By 1944 women constituted around 20% of medical practitioners but from the 1970s the proportion of women entering medical schools increased steadily until they exceeded 50% in 1991. By 2002, 60% of students accepted into UK medical and dental schools were women.[38] But as in the case of BME doctors, the spread of women across the medical specialties has been uneven, as has their take-up of leadership roles. There are, for example, similar proportions of women and non-white doctors particularly in the Senior House Officer Grade. An Audit Commission Report in 1995 also raised the issues of limits to part-time work and exit from and re-entry to training, which have inevitable consequences for women with family commitments. Research into medical school applicants also reveals that women who were not white were less likely to receive an offer than expected.[39] Female BME doctors have thus been doubly disadvantaged by gender and ethnicity in relation to career progression and in problem areas such as recruitment, training and distinction awards. Again, more work is needed to tease out these vectors of difference which have shaped the working lives of BME female doctors.

Identities

Our interviewees have now lived and worked in Britain for several decades and have raised their families in the local culture.

> *My children are very proud, British Muslims ... they don't want to see themselves as Pakistani because they are born and brought up over here ... they want to serve the community on good value system ... [that] me and my wife are trying to give to them i.e. serve the whole British community irrespective of race, religion and ethnicity rather than having a mindset of seeing people as Muslims, English or Pakistanis ... There's a very good column in the National Census form which says British and then they say which ethnicity and I put Pakistani over there.* MA

For our doctors, practising medicine in the NHS has forged an identity which overarches racial and cultural origins.

> *People need to remember that ... [doctors] ... didn't want to serve Pakistan. They didn't want to serve England. They wanted to serve humanity. So, for me ... my identity is my profession ... I want to be seen as a good health professional rather than [being] seen as a good Pakistani or a good British.* MA

> *I'm religious, but for me my job comes first, my patient comes first; if that you can't do as a doctor then you've got to think twice why did you become a doctor?* UP

Holding fast to a professional identity which overrides these other factors of difference has perhaps, been one way for our interviewees to make sense of their lives to date. Many of our doctors entered Britain in high anticipation of working in the world-renowned NHS.

> *I had a very, very high opinion of NHS ... even in those days, the NHS was the envy of the world ... I think I was very impressed with the system, how the health care is given without ability to pay ... I think [it is] still unique in the world and I'm proud of it.* KC

Their concerns for the future now hinge as much on the current dilemmas posed by healthcare reform and changing public expectations of medicine, as on concerns around ethnicity.

> *Health is becoming a commodity and the fragmentation of the whole profession and the whole health care [is] to benefit private sector ... I'm disappointed that NHS is being fragmented and then the health care could become a two-tier.* KC

Public expectation is changing. One of my biggest [worries] for NHS is now I see elderly people; nobody wants to die ... that is a lot of pressure put on the doctors to resuscitate, but that worries me because you know ... I can keep anybody alive as a doctor, but I think we've ... forgotten dignified death. UP

Medicine is still regarded as a prestigious and worthy profession by our interviewees. Nevertheless, they were highly sensitive to the dangers posed to doctors by the increasing regulation of medicine, perhaps because they know better than most, the damage created by unspoken assumptions and prejudices.

What I see in many Trusts is blame culture, and I think that's what saddens me in NHS; ... my son joined medicine in Manchester six years ago; my daughter refused to joined medicine; I cried because I told her it's a wonderful profession, and last year my [other] son joined medicine I cried again because he's a very nice person, and I said look pendulum has swung too far, you make one mistake you may go to jail. So I didn't want him to [join medicine] ... and that saddens me because I was so passionate about this profession. UP

Summary

Our doctors, like the nurses we interviewed, enjoyed the challenges of working in Manchester's diverse racial culture and helping to address the city's huge health inequalities. The biographical details below provide further confirmation that these particular doctors have achieved considerable professional success despite the difficulties they experienced. Their experiences may be untypical there is plenty of research which presents a more negative picture. Nonetheless, they do confirm that:

- BME doctors in Manchester have faced difficulties at every stage of their careers, from recruitment and training, to deployment and promotion.

- Racism in the workplace was a common experience for BME doctors although interviewees often attempted to challenge discrimination.

- Mentors offered invaluable support and advice.

- Professional and social networks like the British International Doctors Association (BIDA; formally the Overseas Doctor's Association) and the British Association for Physicians of Indian Origin (BAPIO) have provided a collective voice for doctors and their families.

- Academic research raised awareness of racial discrimination and became a lever for lobbying institutions like the BMA and the GMC.

- Manchester's record on promotion of BME doctors to leadership positions is generally poor.

Biographies

SATYA CHATTERJEE, OBE was born in Calcutta, India. He graduated from Patna Medical College and then joined the Indian Medical Corps during the Second World War. He moved to England in 1947 to study for his postgraduate degree in medicine. After passing the membership exam of the Royal College of Physicians he took up post as Registrar in Thoracic Medicine at Walker Gate Hospital in Newcastle. In 1950 he became a Senior Registrar at the Manchester Chest Clinic. After a twelve-month Fulbright Fellowship to study chest diseases at the Albany Medical College in the United States, Satya returned to Manchester Baguley Hospital where he built up the new chest clinic that was opened in 1952. In 1963 Satya was appointed Consultant Chest Physician in charge of the Department of Respiratory Physiology at Wythenshawe Hospital. Satya has played a key role in community and race relations. He helped set up the Overseas Doctors Association in 1976 and was heavily involved with the revitalisation of the Manchester Indian Association and the setting up of Ghandi Hall in 1969. He was Chair of the North West Conciliation Committee for Race Relations, and was appointed as an advisor to the Home Office group for race relations between 1976 and 1986. In 1972 he was awarded an OBE. Dr Chatterjee retired as a Senior Consultant in 1987.

SIR NETAR MALLIK was born in Blackburn in 1935. His father had come over from India in 1928, and was the first GP of Indian origin in that part of the North West. Netar graduated from Manchester University Medical School in 1959 and then spent a year working at Harvard University in the United States on cardiac surgery. He returned to Britain and eventually took up a post at the University Department of Medicine in Cardiff specialising in nephrology and dialysis, then in its infancy. While there, he planned the Renal Unit, and was a member of the Ministry of Health's Working Party on Treatment for Renal Failure from 1965 to 1967. Netar returned to Manchester in 1967 taking up the post of Lecturer then Senior Lecturer in Medicine and Associate Director of the Renal Transplantation Unit based at the Manchester Royal Infirmary from 1968. From 1973, as Consultant Renal Physician, Netar developed an internationally recognised Department of Renal Medicine integrated with the Transplantation service in Manchester. Netar has advised the government on renal disease and has been President of the Renal Association of Great Britain and Ireland. He is a Fellow of the Royal College of Physicians (London) and *ad personam* of the Colleges of Physicians of Edinburgh and of Ireland and of the Royal College of Surgeons of Edinburgh. He was also Medical Director of Central Manchester Health Authority between 1997–2000. In 1999, Netar received a knighthood for his services to renal medicine, and in 2002–2003 served as High Sheriff of Greater Manchester, being the first Asian to hold the honorary post. He retired as Professor of Renal Medicine in Manchester in 2000.

KAILASH CHAND was born in Punjab, India, in 1948. After graduating from Patiala Medical College (Punjab) in 1974 he came to England in May 1978 to pursue postgraduate qualification. Kailash worked at Alder Hey Children's Hospital, Liverpool, and Ancoats and Park hospitals in Manchester, and completed a diploma in tropical medicine and health at Liverpool in 1980. He began his GP training in Manchester in the early 1980s and established his own practice in Ashton Under Lyne in 1988. Kailash is active within the BMA and currently serves on a number of committees including the general practitioners committee, the equal opportunities committee, and the international committee. In 2009 he was awarded fellowship of the BMA for his services to professionals and patients. He is Vice-Chair of the Indian Doctors Association, and Vice-Chairman of the International Council of Indian Languages and Culture, which promotes integration and understanding in multiracial Britain. He is a member of the Professional Executive Committee for NHS Tameside and Glossop, Chairman for Tameside and Glossop British Medical Association, and serves as a member of a number of health and scrutiny panels within the local borough. Kailash has written extensively on community health matters in the local, regional and national press. He is retiring from general practice in 2009 but will take up the post of Chair of NHS Tameside and Glossop.

UMESH PRABHU is a Consultant Paediatrician with the Pennine Acute Hospitals NHS Trust. He was born in Mangalore in India. After graduating from medical school in South India in 1980, and completing a diploma in child health, Umesh came to Britain in 1982 to pursue postgraduate qualifications. After training in Paediatrics at Hartlepool, Oxford, Edinburgh and Leeds he was appointed Consultant Paediatrician to the Bury NHS Trust in 1992. Between 1993 and 1998 he was Lead Clinician for Paediatrics at Fairfield General Hospital, Bury. Between 1998 and 2002 Umesh was Medical Director of Bury Health Care NHS Trust. Umesh is specially interested in medical risks and patient safety. Since 2003 he has served as an adviser to the National Clinical Assessment Authority, as a member of the Rochdale PCT PPI Forum, and as a Trustee Of Action Against Medical Accidents. He is also an adviser to the second stage complaints for the Healthcare Commission. Umesh is also a co-opted member of the BMA's equal opportunities committee, is Chairman of his local division of the BMA. He has served as National Vice-Chairman of the British Association of Physicians of Indian Origin (BAPIO), and is currently National Vice-Chairman of the British International Doctors Association (BIDA; formally the Overseas Doctor's Association).

ANEEZ ESMAIL works as a clinician in an inner-city practice in Manchester, and is Professor of General Practice at the University of Manchester. He was born in Kenya in 1957 to second generation East African Asian parents, and lived in Uganda. He attended school in England, and was later joined by the rest of his family after Idi Amin expelled all Ugandan Asians in 1972. Aneez qualified as a medical practitioner from Sheffield University in 1982, and then went on to complete training as a general practitioner in 1987, and as a public health physician in 1992. He obtained his PhD from the University of London in 1996. Between 1996 and 2001, he was Head of the School of Primary Care at the University of Manchester. Aneez has researched extensively on discrimination in the medical profession, particularly around the recruitment, selection and monitoring of the medical profession. In 1997 he was awarded a Harkness Fellowship in international recognition of his work in this area, during which he spent a year as a Visiting Professor at Harvard Medical School. Aneez has also sat on several national working parties looking at the issue of racism in the medical profession, patient safety in primary care, and on the assessment of doctors. He was medical advisor to the Chairman of the Shipman Inquiry between 2001–2004. He was co-Chair of the BMA Equal Opportunities Committee between 2004–2007. He is an active trade unionist and was President of the Medical Practitioners Union between 1997–2003. He is also Associate Vice-President for Equality and Diversity at the University of Manchester.

SYED NAYYER ABIDI was born in Pakistan in 1962. He graduated from Nishtar Medical College, Multan, Pakistan, obtaining his MBBS degree in 1987. He worked as Senior House Surgeon & Registrar in Orthopaedic Surgery and as Medical Officer in General Medicine at Nishtar Hospital, Multan, Pakistan between 1988 and 1991 before coming to the Britain to pursue a postgraduate medical education. Syed completed Surgical Fellowship (FRCS) courses, obtained postgraduate training at Rochdale Infirmary, and has worked at various NHS hospitals, including Tameside General Hospital, Ashton-under-Lyne. Syed currently works as a health promotion specialist in the voluntary sector, conducting a national health awareness project, the M.E.H.A Project, from Hope Hospital, Salford. Launched in February 2002, the project is led by a group of health promoters and aims to provide the latest healthcare information in native languages and raise health awareness mainly in the minority ethnic communities of the UK. Syed is also the author of the UK's first-ever Urdu healthcare book, *Solution to Common Health Issues* (2000) and the UK's first-ever bilingual (English/Urdu) healthcare book, *Prevention is Always Better than Cure* (2002). He was the founding Chief Executive & Media Spokesperson of BEHAF (British Ethnic Health Awareness Foundation), 2003–2006, and is Director General of CHIEF (Community Health Involvement & Empowerment Forum), a social enterprise led by community service users that aims to reduce health inequalities and improve the quality of life of the public, particularly the BME communities of England & Wales. Syed has won numerous awards in recognition of his voluntary work, and was recently elected as a Fellow of the Royal Society for Public Health in recognition of his professional achievements in public health medicine.

MAHMOOD ADIL is currently a Fellow at the NHS Institute for Innovation and Improvement while on secondment from the Department of Health. He was born in Pakistan, and studied medicine at the King Edward Medical University in Lahore, graduating with MBSS in 1987. He then came to England to pursue postgraduate training in public health and obtained his Master of Public Health at the University of Glasgow in 1990. Mahmood trained in paediatrics between 1990 and 1994, and in public health between 1994 and 1999. He was appointed Consultant in Public Health Medicine for the NHS Executive North West in 1999. In 2002 he was appointed Head of Clinical Support and Health Protection for the North West and also Deputy Regional Director of Public Health which he continued until September 2007. In 2005 he held a visiting faculty position in Global Health at Yale University School of Public Health. His most recent position, September 2007 to March 2009, was as Medical Director for the Care Quality Commission Establishment Team based at the Department of Health, London. Mahmood led the health services planning for the 2002 Commonwealth Games held in Manchester. He worked on developing national diabetes policy for England, dealt with the issues relating to poorly performing doctors in collaboration with the General Medical Council, and around the BME health agenda, chaired the North West BME Health Task Force. He holds professional qualifications in medical, health economics, informatics, management and public health fields including Fellowships of the Faculty of Public Health Medicine (London), and of the Royal College of Physicians (Edinburgh). He is a graduate of executive leadership programmes at the Kennedy School of Government (Harvard University), the Judge Institute of Management (University of Cambridge), UK National Common Purpose programme and selected for the Prime Minister's Top Management Programme at the National School of Government. He is also a member of the Peoples University management board to establish a web-based university for low cost public health education for developing countries.

PERIHAN TORUN was born in Istanbul, Turkey, in 1960. She graduated in medicine in Turkey in 1983, and worked for ten years as a GP before moving into public health. In 1996, as part of her training in public health, Perihan came to Britain to conduct observations and clinical attachments at hospitals in Wales, Manchester and Wolverhampton. After moving between Turkey and England, during which time Perihan completed the first year of a two-year Master's Degree in Epidemiology at the London School of Hygiene, she and her family settled in Manchester in 2001. Following this, Perihan completed her Master's Degree, and undertook specialist registrar training in public health in Manchester. Recently she has held the post of Research Associate at Manchester University working on a European Union Project. Perihan is also a member of the UK management team / Educational Oversight and Quality Assurance group for the Peoples University, a web-based university that has been established to provide low cost public health education for developing countries. She also teaches epidemiology and statistics on the Liverpool Masters in Public Health programme and has worked as a volunteer epidemiologist for Doctors Worldwide, a UK-based international medical relief charity.

Learning from the past

It will be clear from the preceding pages that the experiences of the individual BME clinicians we have spoken to, and the many others that they represent, are tightly interwoven with the wider histories of labour shortages, migration, and discrimination, and indeed with the history of medicine and the NHS in Manchester. Yet despite this complex mix of issues across periods and communities there are two pervasive themes which resonate as strongly in 2009 as they have done for decades: health workforce planning and discrimination. In this final chapter we summarise our findings and focus on these key areas, suggesting ways in which our evidence might form a basis for future action.

Health Workforce Planning

Since the 1930s the expansion of UK health services, coupled with imbalances in training numbers for doctors and longstanding difficulties with the recruitment and retention of nurses, has given rise to a series of manpower crises that successive governments have resolved through short-term solutions like recruiting overseas workers. It is clear that any government would find it very difficult to manage health manpower requirements by achieving equilibrium between migration and immigration flows; shortages of health workers, especially doctors, are difficult to handle because of the lag time between the creation of training places and qualification. Nevertheless, it is also clear that a lack of longitudinal data around the migration, immigration, recruitment and retention of health workers has contributed to the difficulties. As indeed has the fact that workforce planning for medicine and nursing have been treated as separate enterprises, despite evidence from economic analysts since the 1960s of the inherent problems in this approach.[1] In May 2006 Josie Irwin, Head of Employment Relations for the Royal College of Nursing summarised the present difficulties in oral evidence to the House of Commons' Health Committee. Numbers of nurses, she said, had increased by 85,000 since 1997. However:

> the quality of workforce planning in the UK means that we do not know where all those nurses have gone; we do not know how many of them have stayed in the UK; we do not know how many of them have stayed in the NHS … we do not know very much about the retirement behaviour of these nurses … the success of importing new numbers of nurses in the UK is challenged by not knowing enough about them once they have entered the workforce.[2]

A recent report by the Organisation for Economic Cooperation and Development (OECD) on *The Looming Crisis in the Health Workforce* suggests that the management of the health workforce is one of the major international challenges of the twenty-first century, particularly as current population projections suggest that many countries will experience a contraction in younger age cohorts and thus the overall pool of potential workers will be diminished. The report recommends that migration and training policies should be undertaken in parallel with other policies such as improving retention, enhancing integration in the workforce, and improving productivity. The way forward, it suggests, is through improved international monitoring of and communication about health workforce policy with the aim of anticipating potential imbalances of demand and supply in the global market.[3] There are indications that action is beginning to be taken. For example in April 2009, the NHS Workforce Review Team and the Institute of Health Sciences at the University of Manchester set up a Special Interest Group to raise the profile of strategic workforce issues and increase scientific knowledge, as well as influence research, education, and future planning: the first seminar will look at global immigration patterns of doctors, nurses and allied health professionals.

The history of BME clinicians is inextricably linked to this wider history of health workforce planning. Since 2000, UK medical and nursing school places have increased significantly and the current political intention is to develop a sustainable UK-trained workforce. Yet over the past decades, unplanned shifts in population growths, upturns and downturns in economic conditions, and changing political motivations have created contingencies in the health workforce for which successive governments were unprepared. There is little to suggest these patterns will change, especially in the context of an international shortage of health workers. Yet although it may not bring future solutions in its wake, mapping what has happened in the past and what is happening in the present could be an effective way of building understanding of the possible options that lie ahead. At the very least it would contribute to our knowledge of the work patterns of BME clinicians and provide an evidence-base from which to monitor equity in training and career progression across race and gender.

Discrimination and BME clinicians

We have clear evidence from our interviewees and from the wider sources used in this study that since the late 1940s, BME nurses, doctors, and other health workers in the UK have experienced institutional discrimination in career development, promotion and training opportunities, as well as social discrimination from patients and colleagues. There is no doubt that however positive the 'spin' put on their experiences and career trajectories, the odds for success were stacked against these BME clinicians. Current statistics suggest that difficulties remain: BME doctors are over-represented in the GMC's disciplinary procedures; and BME clinicians continue to be under-represented in executive, senior professional and support worker positions across NHS organisations. More positively our local history has shown that discrimination is not intransigent: from our interviewees we know that equal opportunities legislation and new recruitment regulations have made recruitment processes more equitable; and from demographic data on medical school entry which shows that BME groups overall are now over-represented amongst medical students, we know that some ethnic groups share the same chances of gaining a place as their white counterparts. What then are the prospects for the future? And how might history help us to identify a way forward?

First and foremost, history can provide the broader context for our present problem of discrimination by embedding it within the wider structures and practices of medicine. Medicine is a social enterprise and necessarily reflects the wider attitudes and understandings of the period. Hence we have many examples within medical history of discrimination against particular groups on the basis of certain characteristics. This is not to suggest that we should accept racial discrimination as a product of our times and retreat from tackling the clear inequities, but rather that we need to tease out the causes and consequences of racial discrimination by mapping the experiences of our individual BME clinicians on to the wider histories of nursing and medicine. We can best understand discrimination, not just as a one-dimensional problem centred on the mass employment of overseas workers in the NHS during the last half of the twentieth century, but rather as a multi-dimensional problem that is, in part, a consequence of the professionalisation of medicine and nursing from the nineteenth century.

As we noted in the introduction, one of the strengths of this study is its inclusive approach to BME clinicians. This has allowed us to identify the many commonalities in experiences between doctors and nurses with regard to institutional discrimination in NHS organisations and social discrimination by patients and colleagues. Our interviewees have shared many similar difficult experiences: adjusting to the UK weather and food; coping with unfair recruitment processes and pressure to work in unpopular specialisms; and not least, enduring the hurt of racial comments. Many interviewees drew support from informal mentors, or organisations like the Overseas Doctors' Association and the British Association for Physicians of Indian Origin. There is consensus that particularly since the 1990s new legislation and workplace regulations have improved matters although difficulties remain. But we have also found significant differences in the histories of the two key occupational groups – nurses and doctors – which relate to the wider histories of nursing and medicine.[4] It is to these differences that we now turn, first in relation to nurses.

Nurses

Nurse shortages have been a perennial problem in the UK since at least the 1930s. Then, Britain looked to recruit nurses from Ireland and Europe to supplement its workforce. The creation of the NHS in 1948 intensified the problems as the spread of specialists and expanding technologies required unprecedented increases in the medical and nursing workforce. Unsurprisingly, many parts of the NHS struggled to recruit enough staff to sustain this expansion. A downturn in Irish migration coupled with new entry procedures for Irish migrants forced Britain to look elsewhere. From this point onwards, the primary strategy used to solve the problem was the recruitment of nurses from overseas, underpinned by campaigns to recruit UK trainees. Certainly these measures have proved effective in the short-term and generally succeeded in limiting the impact on the NHS of nurse shortages. In political terms, overseas recruitment has offered the speediest and most cost-effective way of resolving staffing crises. As recently as 2002, the head of nursing at the Manchester Royal Infirmary confirmed that without the 250 nurses recruited from India, around twenty wards would have closed. Nurse shortages are now an international problem and the UK has not been alone in attempting resolution by looking beyond its shores: in 2002, overseas nurses made up 23% of the nurse workforce in New Zealand; 6% in Canada; 4% in the US; and 8% in Ireland and the UK.[5] Nurse shortages remain a problem – by 2010 the nurse shortfall is anticipated to be 53,000 in the UK, 40,000 in Australia, and 275,000 in the US – suggesting that the strategies employed to date have not remedied the underlying issues associated with recruitment and retention.

The problems of nurse recruitment and retention have been explained across periods and successive crises as stemming from the comparatively low wages, unattractive working conditions, and alternative employment opportunities. We saw earlier how low professional status and marginalisation from medical management has coloured the history of nursing from its beginnings. That nursing was 'by definition *not* medicine' has been central to its ideologies and practices since the nineteenth century.[6] The growing emphasis on academic nursing from the 1970s attempted to 'rebalance' nursing from practical skills towards theoretical knowledge. Project 2000 in the 1980s was an attempt to shift hospitals' dependence on trainee nurse labour and allow trainees more time to learn. However, it also reinforced longstanding divisions between medicine and nursing by claiming that nursing was health-focused whereas medicine was disease-focused. In recent years the expansion of the nurse-practitioner role and the introduction of multi-disciplinary teams have softened these boundaries; many nurse-practitioners now run out-patient clinics where they assess patients and their treatment requirements, and they undertake limited prescribing. Part of the political will for the creation of such posts was the economic benefits: nurse-practitioners are a cheaper resource than doctors. Skills-mix roles like nurse-practitioners may eventually help to reshape divisions of labour between medicine and nursing but change is likely to be incremental rather than revolutionary.

Nursing's subordinate status to medicine and weaker political leverage has also made it difficult for the profession to achieve generous pay settlements, and overseas recruitment has sometimes, as in the 1960s, enabled the government of the day to sidestep UK nurses' pay claims. With the financial pressures on the NHS set to escalate it seems unlikely that nursing will be able to redress this historical set of problems in the near future.

BME nurses seem to have been doubly disadvantaged by the intersection of racial and gender discrimination and the structures and low status of nursing. Many of the nurses who came to the UK from the Caribbean in the 1950s expected to achieve the internationally recognised SRN which would allow them to return home and gain employment. The work of Baxter and Ali has shown us that irrespective of the educational qualifications they had gained in their home country, BME nurses struggled to enter SRN training because contemporaries argued that their racial characteristics limited their intellectual capacities and motivation to achieve that level of training. Thus many overseas nurses were forced or even duped into SEN training rather than the more prestigious and more highly valued SRN qualification. The long-term consequences of this were significant as the SEN was not an internationally recognised qualification and limited overseas nurses' options for returning home.

Within nursing, the two-tier system of SRN and SEN qualifications was used to segregate nurses; SEN nurses of all nationalities were usually channelled into the less popular and prestigious specialties. Our interviewees were exceptional in that they had all trained as SRNs or gained RGN – introduced in 1986. But these higher qualifications did not prevent our nurses experiencing difficulties in gaining promotion or training opportunities, or being pressured to take on night shifts and to work in unpopular areas such as mental health or geriatric nursing. The replacement of the SRN and SEN qualifications in 1986 by the RGN and the post of health assistant seems to have exchanged one two-tier system for another; evidence suggests that health assistants – many of whom are from BME groups – find it difficult to access RGN training. Critics argue that the successive restructuring of nursing has created a small elite 'core' supported by a large peripheral workforce undertaking basic care, thus reinforcing inequalities.[7]

Gender discrimination added an additional layer of difficulty for BME nurses when changes to the RCN's membership rules from the 1960s onwards encouraged the recruitment of more male nurses. We saw earlier how male nurses progressed more rapidly up the nursing hierarchies and dominated the senior posts; other research suggests that the challenges of combining work and family which create periods of career stasis for female nurses incentivise male nurses to intensify their career-building.[8]

Symbolic of the wider problems with low status, has been the reluctance of BME nurses to vocalise their struggles; Baxter's 1988 study was the first to address the particular issues facing BME nurses although we know that problems were evident from the 1950s. Most of our nurse interviewees had received support from informal mentors but BME nurses had no collective mouthpiece through which to pursue BME interests with nursing institutions like the RCN. The absence of group action suggests the fears and vulnerabilities of BME nurses: one of our interviewees had attempted but failed to set up a black nurses' group because her colleagues were 'too scared of losing their jobs'.[9] Since the 1980s the working environment for BME nurses has certainly improved as a result of national legislation on equal opportunities: Baxter's fears that the black nurse could become extinct by the 2000s were not realised. And in 2003, the RCN joined with the NHS Confederation to launch the NHS Black and Minority Ethnic Leadership Forum which aims to spread BME leadership and provide a voice for BME health workers. Yet significant problems remain. BME nurses are under-represented at senior levels and there are a decreasing number of new BME entrants to nursing. One of the most poignant legacies of discrimination that came to light during our study was the tendency of BME nurses to actively discourage their children from entering the profession: 'nursing isn't a job you'd want your daughter to do'.

One of the most positive interventions noted in many of our interviews has been support from mentors. Most importantly, these mechanisms of support legitimised the individual clinician's experiences in the workplace and provided a safe forum in which to explore difficulties. Mentoring schemes are now integrated into NHS structures. In 2004, the north west strategic health authorities, including the Greater Manchester Strategic Health Authority, set up the North West Mentoring Scheme which is 'open to all NHS staff'. However, potential mentees are defined as staff who have 'some managerial or leadership element to their role … [and have] identified mentoring as appropriate through their organisational personal development planning process'.[10] It is possible then that some NHS staff, particularly junior nurses, will not be able to access this scheme if they are deemed not to have the appropriate type of job. One question raised by several of our interviewees was whether successful BME clinicians should be doing more to help others locally in Manchester. Informal mentoring schemes to support BME clinicians who may be excluded from the north west scheme may be one simple, bottom-up action that could help bring about change.

In nursing then, racial discrimination has operated through many inter-related factors: nursing's subordinate position to medicine and low professional status; the internal structures of nursing which have created a workforce fragmented by qualifications and working arrangements; the lack of a collective mouthpiece for BME interests within and beyond nursing and consequent slow uptake of research; and, of course, the wider racist attitudes of the period. We turn now to see how BME doctors have fared in comparison to their nursing counterparts.

Doctors

Since the 1950s, shortages of doctors have also been a recurring problem for the NHS; it has proved difficult to balance medical manpower planning; the migration of UK-trained doctors to other countries; and changing patterns of health services. As with nurse shortages, overseas recruitment has been used by successive governments as the short-term solution to crises. The Indian sub-continent provided an ideal recruitment ground because colonial rule had established Indian medical schools on the UK model, with teaching in English and standards linked to the GMC's requirements. In many senses these overseas doctors were a better 'fit' with the UK than European medical graduates.

Like BME nurses, BME doctors have been disadvantaged by the profession's internal hierarchies which left them working on the geographical and institutional margins of medicine. As migrants, they experienced difficulties in getting shortlisted for jobs and were more likely to gain posts away from prestigious teaching hospitals and medical schools – in hospitals in the poorer parts of the Manchester region, or in single handed GP practices in deprived areas. Some BME doctors even had to accept lower remuneration in order to support themselves and their families. Nor were BME doctors trained in the UK exempt from barriers, particularly around selection processes where those responsible for shortlisting candidates frequently excluded individuals on the basis of a foreign surname.

Entry to the UK became increasingly difficult from the late 1970s onwards because of the tightening of immigration and registration controls. The GMC withdrawal of recognition for Indian colleges' medical qualifications created a two-tier system of 'full' and 'limited' registration in the UK and created problems for doctors who wanted to return to their home country. From 1985, entry for doctors holding career posts depended on gaining a work-permit; those seeking post-graduate training were given an initial period of up to four years, later extended to six.

One of the enduring areas of criticism has centred on BME doctors' communication skills. In the 1970s, difficulties in understanding and speaking the English language were used to justify the lack of career progression and exam failure of overseas doctors, and to underpin accusations that overseas doctors were offering a poor standard of care. The PLAB test was introduced in direct response to these widely publicised comments. By the early 1980s, however, evidence showed that around two-thirds of overseas-qualified doctors had no significant language handicap, and that any initial problems with language were resolved after the first few years in the UK.[11] Nevertheless, the 'myth of language problems became part of the normal discourse' on overseas doctors.[12] Some overseas doctors may have struggled to get to grips with the varied accents and dialects of the UK, but much of the problem, as we learnt from our interviewees, stems from cultural differences in expectations and norms of behaviour in doctor–nurse and doctor–patient relationships. Body language and tone of voice convey subtle messages about relationships and identities and it seems that some overseas doctors were accustomed to behaving in a more autocratic fashion with nurses and patients than was the custom in the UK. Some of our interviewees were fortunate enough to be enlightened to the difficulties by friendly colleagues and swiftly adapted their behaviour. A current article by Parinthia on the BAPIO website gives evidence of the continuing challenges of adapting to a different medical environment:

> In what way is clinical practice in [the] UK different than our home country? Is it completely different or is it just that things are better defined? The latter seems to be more appropriate. The approach to clinical practice is very patient-oriented; be it patient confidentiality or data protection or even practice of evidence-based medicine. There is more emphasis to Clinical Governance, Multidisciplinary team approach, Communication skills and Continuous Professional Development of the staff. All these may sound very different initially and one may question the need; but this is what makes NHS to be one of the best health organisations of the world.[13]

The elements of biomedicine – knowledge of the causation, modes of transmission, prevention, and treatment of disease – can be taught in medical schools around the world and yet the practice of medicine depends on applying this knowledge across an intricate web of social practices and behaviours. The over-representation of BME doctors in the GMC's disciplinary proceedings may well be a result of these sorts of complex and intangible difficulties rather than more clear-cut definitions of poor practice. It seems likely that some of these problems will resolve with time as more second-generation BME doctors join the profession.

Yet overall, BME doctors seem to have fared better within their profession than BME nurses, partly because they developed a collective voice and became politically active. The Overseas Doctors' Association was established in Manchester in 1976, soon after the publication of the Merrison Report which was one of the first to criticise standards of skills and care in overseas doctors. The ODA was politically active from the beginning, rebuffing criticisms about the qualifications and training of overseas doctors, and collaborating closely with researchers who began to provide evidence of the barriers encountered by BME doctors in training and career progression. The development of a sound evidence-base has been significant in raising awareness of the problems of BME doctors, and in facilitating engagement with medical institutions like the GMC and the medical colleges. The political advantages of such representative groups was highlighted in 2008 when BAPIO's challenge in the High Court about new Department of Health rules which sought retrospectively to debar IMGs from applying from training posts was upheld by the House of Lords.

The ODA and BAPIO have also been and remain sources of practical advice for individual overseas doctors and their families, often arranging social events as well as providing professional support. As with the earlier development of specialist medical societies in the UK, the formation of these groups has helped to secure BME identities across medical networks.

That BME doctors have overcome some of the barriers against them is evidenced by recent data on the demography of medical schools. White British and Asian British applicants to medical school share the same chance of success in gaining a place. In part, this has to be seen as a positive legacy of BME doctor-activist groups which have lobbied medical schools since the 1980s, using research evidence to show how recruitment processes are key to equity across ethnic groups. The differential acceptance rate across ethnic groups suggests that discrimination may still be problematic for some BME applicants, but the difficulties are also closely linked to social class. Recent research has confirmed that the social class of medical students has changed little over the past decades: the majority come from professional and managerial backgrounds. Given the difference between social backgrounds of the different ethnic groups – white, black, and Indian medical school applicants tend to be of a higher social class than applicants from Bangladeshi, Chinese, and Pakistani communities – applicants from the lower social class ethnic groups may be disadvantaged by class factors rather than ethnicity. Medical schools have acknowledged their social responsibility to try to ensure that the gender, ethnicity and socio-economic backgrounds of medical students should mirror the multiracial society that they will serve when qualified. And in recent years, the Widening Participation scheme run by universities has focused attention on the need to encourage under-represented social groups to participate in higher education. Reforming recruitment processes have been a key part of these initiatives.

Since the 1990s, recruitment processes in medical schools and across NHS trusts have become more robust. Many NHS human resources departments have introduced anonymous selection procedures so that applications are tagged with a number rather than the name of the applicant. There is still scope however for scrutiny of the processes of selection panels and for ensuring that members are fully aware of the issues around discrimination. The new Equalities Bill which was introduced in April 2009 promotes fairness and equality of opportunity and introduces transparency into the workplace. It requires public bodies to consider the diverse needs and requirements of their workforce when developing employment policies and planning services. BME clinicians may benefit from some of these measures but positive discrimination is problematical. The evidence suggests that most BME clinicians would prefer to get a job on the basis of merit rather than ethnicity as indeed would women in medicine who are also targets for positive gender discrimination.

Most tellingly, our interviewees identified themselves first and foremost as doctors. This professional identity came above ethnic and cultural identities and expresses the passion and commitment these doctors feel for the NHS. It is also what enabled them to meet the many challenges of establishing careers in Britain. Despite all the difficulties, the NHS is still regarded as the best health-care system and continues to attract overseas-trained doctors. The reason for the NHS' popularity, explained a German-trained junior doctor in 2004, was that 'in the UK, advice from even very distinguished doctors is easy to obtain and there is rarely any hesitation in engaging in an educative conversation'.[14]

The way forward

Despite the continuing difficulties that face BME clinicians it would be wrong to conclude on a pessimistic note. Using history as a critical tool in this fraught arena is helpful in three ways. First, it offers hope by showing how some of the barriers faced by BME clinicians, especially doctors, have been overcome; second, it reveals the problems which persist in Manchester and beyond and continue to require attention; and third, learning from what has been helpful in improving equity and opportunity in the past has enabled us to identify several areas at local, national, and global levels where action could make a difference.

1. *Manpower Planning*

- Unplanned shifts in demographics, economic conditions and political motivations have created contingencies in health manpower planning for which successive governments were unprepared.

- There has been a failure to collect longitudinal data that might help anticipate impending crises and map recruitment and retention patterns. Such data would make it easier to identify inequity in training and career progression in BME clinicians.

- The management of the health workforce is an international challenge, particularly as current population projections suggest that many countries will experience a contraction in younger age cohorts and the overall pool of potential workers will be diminished.

2. *Support Systems*

- Mentors have provided positive support which legitimises the BME clinician's experiences in the workplace and provides a safe forum in which to reflect on difficulties. It is essential that all levels of BME clinicians should have access to these support systems.

- Evidence-based research into discrimination has been an effective mechanism for achieving change and has helped mobilise debate on the issues.

3. *Career Training and Progression*

- Equal opportunities legislation and changes to recruitment processes in medical schools have brought improved equity of opportunity although some BME groups still experience discrimination.

- British Asian medical school applicants share equal chances of acceptance as white British students although some BME groups continue to experience difficulties. More research is needed into the interplay between ethnicity, social class and gender in medical school demography.

- Communication difficulties are likely to ease over time because the second generation have been brought up within UK culture.

- New legislation like the Equalities Bill should be monitored to ensure that it is not creating unanticipated and unwanted consequences.

4. Integration not segregation

- Discrimination must be seen as a shared problem for all NHS employees across race, gender and socio-economic status.

- Many BME clinicians prioritise their professional identity and this could be used as a means of strengthening collegial working practices.

Appendices

Appendix 1   Breakdown of ethnicity of workforce by staff group in Manchester NHS Trusts 2008/2009

(*Source*: Data provided by NHS Trusts under Freedom of Information.)

a. Central Manchester and Manchester Children's University Hospitals NHS Foundation Trust

Ethnic Origin	Add profes-sional & Scientific	Add clinical Support Services	Administration and Mgrs	AHPs	Estates	Healthcare Scientists	Medical & Dental	Nursing Professionals	Students
White British	82.3%	79.3%	85.0%	85.0%	61.0%	83.8%	47.1%	73.2%	64.3%
Irish	1.6%	1.8%	1.4%	3.3%	2.7%	1.3%	1.8%	2.0%	0.0%
Any other White background	1.6%	1.5%	1.7%	1.1%	0.1%	3.1%	9.0%	0.8%	0.0%
White and Black Caribbean	0.3%	1.2%	0.3%	0.3%	0.0%	0.7%	0.1%	0.1%	0.0%
White and Black African	0.5%	0.8%	0.3%	0.0%	0.3%	0.4%	0.7%	0.6%	0.0%
White and Asian	0.5%	0.3%	0.3%	0.0%	0.0%	0.4%	0.7%	0.0%	0.0%
Any other mixed background	0.0%	0.6%	0.3%	0.8%	0.1%	0.2%	0.4%	0.2%	0.0%
Indian	2.2%	2.2%	1.7%	1.4%	2.7%	1.1%	17.8%	12.1%	7.1%
Pakistani	1.1%	1.1%	0.9%	1.7%	0.8%	2.7%	5.5%	0.9%	0.0%
Bangladeshi	0.0%	0.1%	0.3%	0.0%	0.4%	0.2%	0.3%	0.2%	0.0%
Any other Asian background	0.5%	0.4%	0.2%	0.6%	0.0%	0.9%	2.5%	0.6%	0.0%
Caribbean	0.0%	0.8%	0.3%	0.0%	5.2%	0.0%	0.4%	0.3%	0.0%
African	1.4%	1.4%	0.8%	0.8%	11.3%	1.3%	2.3%	2.7%	0.0%
Any other Black background	0.5%	1.1%	0.2%	0.0%	3.8%	0.2%	0.1%	0.3%	0.0%
Chinese	0.8%	0.2%	0.2%	0.3%	0.8%	0.9%	3.0%	0.4%	0.0%
Any other Ethnic Group	0.8%	1.0%	0.7%	0.3%	9.5%	0.5%	2.5%	0.5%	0.0%
Not Stated	5.7%	6.5%	5.3%	4.4%	1.4%	2.5%	5.8%	4.9%	28.6%

b. University Hospital of South Manchester NHS Foundation Trust

Ethnic Origin	Add Prof, Scientific & Technic	Additional Clinical Services	Administrative and Clerical	Allied Health Professionals	Estates & Ancillary	Healthcare Scientists	Medical & Dental	Nursing and Midwifery Registered	Students
White-British	89.5%	79.7%	89.0%	89.2%	87.1%	87.5%	57.4%	74.6%	80.0%
White-Irish	0.8%	3.0%	1.4%	1.4%	0.0%	1.0%	2.2%	2.6%	0.0%
White-Any other White Background	1.7%	2.1%	0.3%	2.2%	0.0%	1.0%	4.4%	1.4%	20.0%
White Northern Irish	0.0%	0.0%	0.0%	0.0%	0.0%	0.0%	0.2%	0.0%	0.0%
White Unspecified	0.0%	0.0%	0.1%	0.0%	0.0%	0.0%	0.0%	0.0%	0.0%
White Greek	0.0%	0.0%	0.0%	0.0%	0.0%	0.0%	0.2%	0.0%	0.0%
White Polish	0.0%	0.3%	0.0%	0.0%	0.0%	0.0%	0.0%	0.1%	0.0%
White ex-USSR	0.0%	0.1%	0.0%	0.0%	0.0%	0.0%	0.0%	0.0%	0.0%
Mixed-White and Black Caribbean	0.0%	0.3%	0.2%	0.0%	0.0%	0.0%	0.2%	0.1%	0.0%
Mixed-White and Black African	0.0%	0.3%	0.0%	0.0%	0.0%	0.0%	0.5%	0.8%	0.0%
Mixed-White and Asian	0.0%	0.5%	0.1%	0.0%	0.0%	0.0%	0.5%	0.2%	0.0%
Mixed-Any other mixed background	0.0%	0.0%	0.3%	0.0%	0.0%	0.0%	0.2%	0.2%	0.0%
Asian or Asian British-Indian	0.8%	1.3%	1.0%	1.8%	0.0%	1.0%	12.8%	7.6%	0.0%
Asian or Asian British-Pakistani	1.3%	0.4%	0.7%	0.0%	0.0%	2.1%	6.1%	0.8%	0.0%
Asian or Asian British-Bangladeshi	0.8%	0.1%	0.0%	0.0%	0.0%	0.0%	0.7%	0.1%	0.0%
Asian or Asian British-Any other Asian background	0.0%	0.3%	0.2%	0.7%	0.0%	0.0%	3.9%	0.9%	0.0%
Asian East African	0.0%	0.0%	0.0%	0.0%	0.0%	0.0%	0.2%	0.0%	0.0%
Asian Caribbean	0.4%	1.6%	0.5%	0.4%	3.2%	0.0%	0.0%	1.3%	0.0%

Ethnic Origin	Add Prof, Scientific & Technic	Additional Clinical Services	Administrative and Clerical	Allied Health Professionals	Estates & Ancillary	Healthcare Scientists	Medical & Dental	Nursing and Midwifery Registered	Students
Asian Unspecified	0.0%	0.0%	0.0%	0.0%	0.0%	0.0%	0.2%	0.0%	0.0%
Black or Black British-Caribbean	0.0%	0.1%	0.1%	0.4%	0.0%	0.0%	0.0%	0.2%	0.0%
Black or Black British-African	0.0%	1.0%	0.6%	0.4%	0.0%	3.1%	1.7%	2.8%	0.0%
Black or Black British-Any other Black background	0.0%	0.5%	0.4%	0.0%	0.0%	1.0%	0.0%	0.5%	0.0%
Black Nigerian	0.0%	0.1%	0.0%	0.0%	0.0%	0.0%	0.0%	0.0%	0.0%
Black unspecified	0.4%	0.0%	0.0%	0.0%	0.0%	0.0%	0.0%	0.0%	0.0%
Chinese	0.4%	0.1%	0.1%	0.0%	0.0%	0.0%	1.5%	0.6%	0.0%
Any other Ethnic Group	0.8%	0.1%	0.5%	1.1%	3.2%	1.0%	4.4%	1.1%	0.0%
Malaysian	0.0%	0.0%	0.0%	0.0%	0.0%	0.0%	0.0%	0.1%	0.0%
Not Stated	2.9%	8.0%	4.6%	2.5%	6.5%	2.1%	2.7%	4.1%	0.0%

c. Manchester Mental Health and Social Care NHS Trust

Ethnic Origin	Prof & Tech	Clinical Support Staff	Admin and Clerical	AHPs	Medical & Dental	Nurse & Midwifery	Student Nurses
White	84.81%	75.07%	88.85%	87.93%	76.47%	77.51%	100.00%
Mixed	1.27%	3.25%	0.34%	0.00%	5.88%	2.01%	0.00%
Asian	2.53%	5.42%	3.38%	0.00%	38.24%	1.46%	0.00%
Black	1.27%	7.05%	1.69%	0.00%	11.76%	7.50%	0.00%
Chinese	0.00%	0.27%	0.00%	0.00%	0.00%	0.55%	0.00%
Other Ethnic Group	1.27%	0.27%	0.68%	1.72%	5.88%	0.18%	0.00%
Not Stated	8.86%	8.67%	5.07%	10.34%	26.47%	10.79%	0.00%

d. Pennine Acute Hospitals NHS Trust

Ethnic Origin	Add Clinical Services	Add Prof, Scientific and Tech	Admin & Clerical	AHPs	Estates and Ancillary	Healthcare Scientists	Medical and Dental	Nursing & Midwifery Registered	Students
White-British	92.1%	89.3%	92.8%	90.0%	88.9%	85.6%	37.2%	84.1%	81.8%
White – Irish	1.5%	0.9%	0.8%	0.7%	1.4%	0.7%	1.3%	1.4%	0.0%
White-Any other White Background	0.8%	0.9%	0.6%	1.4%	2.5%	0.7%	5.8%	0.8%	0.0%
Mixed-White & Black Caribbean	0.1%	0.0%	0.3%	0.2%	0.0%	0.4%	0.2%	0.3%	0.0%
Mixed-White & Black African	0.2%	0.0%	0.1%	0.2%	0.1%	0.4%	0.4%	0.3%	0.0%
Mixed-White & Asian	0.3%	0.0%	0.1%	0.2%	0.2%	0.0%	0.5%	0.3%	0.0%
Mixed-Any other Mixed Background	0.0%	0.0%	0.2%	0.2%	0.0%	0.0%	1.5%	0.2%	0.0%
Asian or Asian British-Indian	0.2%	0.9%	0.6%	1.2%	1.3%	1.5%	24.6%	2.0%	0.0%
Asian or Asian British-Pakistani	1.4%	3.7%	1.7%	2.1%	0.6%	5.1%	9.6%	1.5%	0.0%
Asian or Asian British-Bangladeshi	0.1%	1.4%	0.5%	0.9%	0.7%	1.1%	0.9%	0.3%	0.0%
Asian or Asian British-Any other Asian Background	0.3%	0.5%	0.3%	0.0%	0.2%	1.1%	2.6%	2.7%	0.0%
Black or Black British-Caribbean	0.2%	0.0%	0.2%	0.4%	0.3%	0.0%	0.0%	0.3%	0.0%
Black or Black British-African	0.5%	0.5%	0.5%	0.4%	1.1%	2.6%	3.5%	1.8%	0.0%
Black or Black British-Any other Black Background	0.2%	0.0%	0.0%	0.0%	0.2%	0.0%	0.3%	0.5%	0.0%
Chinese	0.0%	0.5%	0.1%	0.2%	0.1%	0.4%	2.3%	0.2%	0.0%
Any other Ethnic Group	0.3%	0.5%	0.3%	0.2%	0.8%	0.0%	6.7%	1.2%	0.0%
Not Stated	1.8%	0.95	0.9%	1.7%	1.6%	0.4%	2.6%	2.1%	18.2%

e. Manchester NHS Primary Care Trust

Ethnic Origin	Add Prof Scientific &Technic	Add Clinical Services	Admin & Clerical	AHPs	Estates and Ancillary	Healthcare Scientists	Medical & Dental	Nursing & Midwifery Registered	Students
White-British	87.20%	84.82%	79.44%	86.16%	84.21%	67.00%	54.16%	85.57%	72.70%
White-Irish	0.00%	1.78%	1.44%	1.97%	5.26%	33.00%	5.20%	2.64%	0.00%
White-Any other White background	0.00%	1.19%	2.27%	3.16%	0.00%	0.00%	3.12%	1.08%	0.00%
White-English	0.00%	0.00%	0.20%	0.00%	0.00%	0.00%	0.00%	0.12%	9.10%
White-Welsh	0.00%	0.00%	0.10%	0.00%	0.00%	0.00%	0.00%	0.00%	0.00%
White Cypriot (non specific)	0.00%	0.00%	0.00%	0.39%	0.00%	0.00%	0.00%	0.00%	0.00%
White Polish	0.00%	0.00%	0.20%	0.00%	0.00%	0.00%	0.00%	0.00%	0.00%
White ex-USSR	0.00%	0.00%	0.10%	0.00%	0.00%	0.00%	0.00%	0.00%	0.00%
White Other European	0.00%	0.00%	0.20%	0.00%	0.00%	0.00%	0.00%	0.00%	0.00%
Mixed-White & Black Caribbean	0.00%	1.19%	1.44%	0.00%	0.00%	0.00%	0.00%	0.48%	0.00%
Mixed-White & Black African	0.00%	0.29%	1.03%	0.39%	5.26%	0.00%	0.00%	0.36%	0.00%
Mixed-White & Asian	0.00%	0.00%	0.41%	0.39%	0.00%	0.00%	0.00%	0.36%	0.00%
Mixed-Any other Mixed background	0.00%	0.00%	0.20%	0.39%	0.00%	0.00%	1.04%	0.12%	0.00%
Asian or Asian British-Indian	0.00%	1.48%	1.13%	0.39%	0.00%	0.00%	14.58%	1.08%	9.10%
Asian or Asian British-Pakistani	0.00%	1.78%	2.68%	0.79%	0.00%	0.00%	6.25%	0.12%	0.00%
Asian or Asian British-Bangladeshi	0.00%	0.00%	0.41%	0.00%	0.00%	0.00%	0.00%	0.12%	0.00%
Asian or Asian British-Any other Asian background	2.56%	0.00%	0.30%	0.39%	0.00%	0.00%	1.04%	0.12%	0.00%
Asian-Caribbean	2.56%	0.89%	0.82%	0.00%	0.00%	0.00%	0.00%	0.60%	0.00%

Ethnic Origin	Add Prof Scientific &Technic	Add Clinical Services	Admin & Clerical	AHPs	Estates and Ancillary	Healthcare Scientists	Medical & Dental	Nursing & Midwifery Registered	Students
Black or Black British-Caribbean	0.00%	2.67%	1.65%	0.00%	5.26%	0.00%	0.00%	0.72%	0.00%
Black or Black British-African	0.00%	0.59%	1.13%	0.39%	0.00%	0.00%	0.00%	1.08%	0.00%
Black or Black British-Any other Black background	0.00%	0.00%	0.82%	0.00%	0.00%	0.00%	0.00%	0.48%	0.00%
Black Somali	0.00%	0.00%	0.10%	0.00%	0.00%	0.00%	0.00%	0.00%	0.00%
Black Nigerian	0.00%	0.00%	0.10%	0.00%	0.00%	0.00%	0.00%	0.00%	0.00%
Black British	0.00%	0.00%	0.10%	0.00%	0.00%	0.00%	0.00%	0.00%	0.00%
Chinese	2.56%	0.00%	0.41%	0.79%	0.00%	0.00%	2.08%	0.12%	0.00%
Any other Ethnic Group	2.56%	0.89%	1.54%	0.00%	0.00%	0.00%	5.20%	0.72%	0.00%
Not Stated	2.56%	2.38%	1.65%	4.34%	0.00%	0.00%	7.29%	4.08%	9.10%

Appendix 2   Timeline

1944 Manchester Guardian reported on 16 August that 63 coloured girls, first contingent of coloured nurses, arrived at a Scottish port from the US.

1948 Recruitment of nurses from Ireland to Manchester hospitals continues; 500 workers from the Caribbean arrive in Britain on the Empire Windrush.

1949 Ministries of Health and Labour (including Colonial Office, General Nursing Council, Royal College of Nursing) start recruitment programme, especially in West Indies. Eg. Barbados Beacon advertises for nursing auxiliaries in British hospitals, including Manchester. Manchester agrees to employ 6 Barbadian women as domestic workers – 4 at the Manchester Royal Infirmary and 2 at Ancoats Hospital. A number of those recruited go on to train as nurses but not in Manchester. Most later return to the Caribbean.

1951 Chief Nursing Officer goes to Caribbean to recruit women workers for NHS.

1952 US passes new immigration laws making it more difficult for Caribbean workers to gain entry there.

1955 Nurses in Huddersfield object to employment of coloured nurses on economic grounds. Leeds Regional Hospital Board reported to be bringing in 29 student nurses from Nigeria and Jamaica.

1958 Race riots in London and Nottingham. West Indian Standing Conference established to promote interests of workers in the UK.

1960 Immigration to Britain from South Asia starts to equal that from the Caribbean.

1961 NHS begins recruiting doctors from India and Pakistan. Daily Mirror reported that in Manchester, one in two doctors are coloured; Manchester Colonial Club (run by coloured immigrants for white boys and girls) the coloured children gave a party for their white friends – Jamaican railway worker Aston Gore dressed up as Santa to give out presents.

1962 Commonwealth Immigrants Act ends open access for Commonwealth citizens. New system of employment vouchers introduced, limiting entry to skilled and professional people.

1963 18,000 doctors recruited from India and Pakistan following Enoch Powell's 10 year community plan. Numbers of West Indian migrants start to fall.

1964 First black matron, Daphne Steele, St Winifred's Hospital, West Yorkshire.

1965 Race Relations Act – defined racial discrimination as treating one person less favourably than another on grounds of colour, race, or ethnic/national origins. Became a breach of civil law to refuse access on racial grounds eg. to public places. Annual limit of 8,500 employment vouchers, mainly skilled and professional workers.

1966 Race Relations Board established to oversee the legislation: set up local committees to investigate complaints and agree settlements.

1967 PC Norwell Roberts became London's first black police officer.

1968 Commonwealth Immigrants Act imposes further controls on immigration; Race Relations Act widened anti-discrimination laws and created the Community Relations Commission; 20 April Enoch Powell gave 'rivers of blood' speech which called for immigration to be reduced immediately.

British Nursing Association (private nurses' agency) said: 'It's useless for us to have coloured nurses on our books in London because there are no positions for them … patients object to being nursed by coloured girls'.

1969 BME nurses make up 25% NHS hospital staff

1970 Royal College of Nursing admits SENs and pupil nurses.

1971 Immigration Act establishes 'partiality' right of immigration restricted to those whose parents/grandparents were born in Britain. 12% of NHS nurses are Irish.

1972 Idi Amin expels Asians from Uganda; 30,000 come to Britain. 'Raise the Roof' campaign by ancillary nursing staff including BME nurses.

1974 Caribbean migration to Britain ceases; immigration from India, Pakistan and Bangladesh continues but at a reduced rate.

1976 Overseas Doctors' Association is established.

Race Relations Act but NHS and Police Force exempt: extended 1968 Act and defined two forms of discrimination, direct and indirect; Commission for Racial Equality established, replacing the Race Relations Board and the Community Relations Commission; Notting Hill riots.

1980 Valerie Bartley won £100 compensation at industrial tribunal over discrimination by Elms Rest Home in Manchester. She said she had worked in two Manchester hospitals without any problems.

1981 Riots in Brixton, the West Midlands, Leeds, Liverpool and Manchester. A response to over 20 years of racism, discrimination, poverty and oppressive policing in the inner cities.

1982 NHS nurses strike over low pay.

1984 Commission for Racial Equality report shows that overseas-born and migrant health workers are concentrated in local status jobs and unpopular fields like geriatric and mental hospitals.

1995 Report on Nursing in a Multi-Ethnic NHS by Policy Studies Institute found widespread racial abuse of black and Asian nurses.

1996 MP Diane Abbott causes controversy by criticising employment of Finnish nurses 'blonde and blue-eyed' rather than Caribbean nurses who 'know the language and understand British culture and institutions' in Homerton Hospital, Hackney.

1998 Fillipino nurses recruited to NHS; TUC conference on black women and the labour market; Government launches document on action to be taken to tackle racial harassment in the NHS.

2002 Highly Skilled Migrant programme: points-based system to allow migrants with certain skills to enter Britain. Sir Magdi Yacoub appointed Special Envoy to the NHS.

2004 Recruitment from abroad continues: dentists from India and Poland; GPs from Spain and Italy; psychiatrists and nurses from India.

2008 Percentage of BME NHS staff is same percentage as in British population, but still fewer representatives in higher levels of the service.

Appendix 3   List of recorded interviews

We would like to thank all those who agreed to be interviewed and recorded for this book. Where agreed, tapes and transcripts have been deposited at the Centre for the History of Science Technology and Medicine and will be made available for further research.

Unless otherwise indicated all interviews were conducted by Emma Jones.

Syed Nayyer Abidi
Mahmood Adil
Carol Baxter
Kailash Chand
Satya Chatterjee
Remi Clarke
Jannett Creese
Jasmine Edwards
Aneez Esmail
Neisha Fielder
Michelle Haller
Sir Netar Malik
Gassim Mohammed
Christine Pearson
Umesh Prabhu (Interviewed by Stephanie Snow)
Gulab Singh
Perihan Torun
Angela Wood

Notes

CHAPTER 1: INTRODUCTION

1. The predominant term employed throughout this book is 'black and minority ethnic', or BME, to describe all members of minority racial groups. Other terms such as 'black', 'West Indian', 'Caribbean', 'Afro-Caribbean', and 'South Asian' and 'Asian' have been used where appropriate to distinguish between ethnic minority groups, and to reflect both the terminology used at the time, and that of our interviewees. We recognise that the persons to whom the terms are applied do not necessarily define themselves by such terms.
2. We have not had the time or resources to address the histories of the large numbers of BME ancillary workers in the NHS during the period.
3. For the event report and photographic timeline see the North West Strategic Health Authority website at www.northwest.nhs.uk/whatwedo/equalityanddiversity/the 60th anniversary of the nhs.html, (accessed 29 September 2009).
4. C. Baxter, *The Black Nurse: An Endangered Species* (Cambridge, 1988), p. 22.
5. J. Bornat, L. Henry and P. Rahjuram, '"Don't mix race with the specialty": Interviewing South Asian Overseas-trained Geriatricians', *Oral History*, 37:1 (2009), pp. 74–84.

CHAPTER 2: POST–WAR BRITAIN: LABOUR AND IMMIGRATION

1. R. Klein, *The New Politics of the NHS: From Creation to Reinvention* (Oxon, 2006), p. 1.
2. C. Webster, *The Health Services Since the War: Government and Health Care. The National Health Service 1958–1979* (London, 1996), Volume 2, p. 21.
3. A. Kramer, *Many Rivers to Cross: The History of the Caribbean Contribution to the NHS* (London, 2006), p. 15.
4. Kramer, *Many Rivers to Cross*, p. 15; V. Berridge, *Health and Society in Britain Since 1939* (Cambridge, 1999), p. 24.

5. Berridge, *Health and Society*, p. 24.

6. Klein, *The New Politics of the NHS*, p. 25.

7. Webster, *The Health Services Since the War*, Volume II, p. 17.

8. D. Kay and R. Miles, *Refugees or Migrant Workers? European Volunteer Workers in Britain, 1946–1951* (London, 1992), p. 15.

9. P. Summerfield, *Reconstructing Women's Wartime Lives: Discourse and Subjectivity in Oral Histories of the Second World War* (Manchester, 1998), ch. 6.

10. Kay and Miles, *Refugees*, pp. 18–19.

11. C. W. Tate, *Leadership in Nursing* (Edinburgh, 1999), p. 182.

12. Kay and Miles, *Refugees*, p. 29.

13. C. S. Chatterton, '"The weakest link in the chain of nursing": Recruitment and Retention in Mental Health Nursing 1948–1968', PhD Thesis, University of Salford (2007), p. 187.

14. Kay and Miles, *Refugees*, p. 74.

15. Ministry of Health, Department of Health for Scotland, and Ministry of Labour and National Service, *Report of the Working Party on the Recruitment and Training of Nurses* (London, 1947), pp. 71–74.

16. Ministry of Health, *Report of the Working Party on the Recruitment and Training of Nurses*, p. 20.

17. D. Mitchell, '"No claim to be called sick nurses at all": An Historical Study of Learning Disability Nursing', PhD Thesis, London South Bank University (2000) p. 191; Chatterton, 'Recruitment and Retention in Mental Health Nursing', p. 4.

18. Kramer, *Many Rivers to Cross*, p. 15; Chatterton, 'Recruitment and Retention in Mental Health Nursing', p. 192.

19. L. Doyal, G. Hunt, and J. Mellor, 'Your Life in their Hands: Migrant Workers in the National Health Service', *Critical Social Policy*, 1 (1981), p. 55.

20. Kay and Miles, *Refugees*, p. 42.

21. Kay and Miles, *Refugees*, pp. 52 and 68.

22. Chatterton, 'Recruitment and Retention in Mental Health Nursing', p. 193.

23. Chatterton, 'Recruitment and Retention in Mental Health Nursing', pp. 194–200.

24. Kay and Miles, *Refugees*, p. 39.

25. P. Fryer, *Staying Power: The History of Black People in Britain* (London, 1984), p. 372.

26. Fryer, *Staying Power*, p. 373.

27. Fryer, *Staying Power*, p. 374.

28. Fryer, *Staying Power*, p. 373.

29. Kramer, *Many Rivers to Cross*, p. 15.

30. Kramer, *Many Rivers to Cross*, p. 17.

31. Kramer, *Many Rivers to Cross*, p. 17.

32. 'Jamaican Nurses are asked to Return Home', *Manchester Guardian*, 24 November 1965, p. 18.

33. Baxter, *The Black Nurse*, p. 14.

34. National Health Service History website, http://www.nhshistory.

net/Chapter%201.htm#Medical_education_and_staffing (accessed 29
September 2009).

35. Great Britain, Committee to Consider the Future Numbers of
Medical Practitioners and Appropriate Intake of Medical Students,
*Report of the Committee to Consider the Future Numbers of Medical
Practitioners and Appropriate Intake of Medical Students* (London, 1957).

36. K. Decker, 'Overseas Doctors: Past and Present' in N. Coker (ed.)
Racism in Medicine: An Agenda for Change (London, 2001), p. 26.

37. A. Esmail, 'Asian Doctors in the NHS: Service and Betrayal (William
Pickles Lecture)', *British Journal of General Practice* (October 2007),
p. 828.

38. On early pioneers see Esmail, 'Asian Doctors', pp. 828–829.

39. R. Visram, *Asians in Britain: 400 Years of History* (London, 2002),
p. 281.

40. Esmail, 'Asian Doctors', p. 829.

41. Esmail, 'Asian Doctors', p. 830.

42. P. Foot, *The Rise of Enoch Powell* (Harmondsworth, 1969), p. 38.

43. Decker, 'Overseas Doctors', p. 25.

44. R. Klein, 'Medical Practice. Contemporary Themes. Medical Manpower I: How much can ancillaries take over', *British Medical Journal*,
(3 January 1976), pp. 25–26, Decker; 'Overseas Doctors', p. 29.

45. J. Seale, 'Medical Emigration from Great Britain and Ireland', *British
Medical Journal*, 1 (1964), p. 1178.

46. 'Looking at the National Health Service', Focus, 5 December 1967,
Radio 4, General Medical Services Committee, 1967–1968, BMA
Archives.

47. Information taken from the 'Moving Here' website, at www.
movinghere.org.uk.

48. A. Marr, *A History of Modern Britain*, (Basingstoke, 2007), p. 40.

49. D. Kynaston, *Austerity Britain, 1945–51* (London, 2007), p. 346.

50. Fryer, *Staying Power*, pp. 376–381.

51. For more information see the Moving Here website: http://www.
movinghere.org.uk/galleries/histories/caribbean/growing_up/
growing_up.htm#schooldays and http://www.movinghere.org.uk/
galleries/histories/asian/growing_up/growing_up.htm#education
(accessed 29 September 2009).

52. Fryer, *Staying Power*, p. 381.

53. R. Sales, *Understanding Immigration and Refugee Policy: Contradictions and
Continuities* (Bristol, 2007), p. 142.

54. R. Hansen, 'The Kenyan Asians, British Politics, and the
Commonwealth Immigrants Act, 1968', *The Historical Journal*, 42:3
(1999), p. 810.

55. Sales, *Understanding Immigration*, pp. 142–143.

56. Sales, *Understanding Immigration*, p. 143.

57. A. Ellis, 'UK Resident Population by Country of Birth', *Population
Trends*, 135 (2009), p. 21.

58. Parliamentary Office of Science and Technology, 'Ethnicity and
Health', *Postnote*, 276 (January 2007), p. 1.

59. C. Webster, *The Health Service Since the War. Volume II*, p. 173.

60. M. Lee-Cunnin, *Daughters of Seacole: A Study of Black Nurses in West Yorkshire* (Batley, 1989), p. 4.

61. J. Hallam, *Nursing the Image: Media, Culture and Professional Identity* (London, 2000), pp. 119–120.

62. The Royal College of Nursing and National Council of Nurses of the United Kingdom, *RCN Evidence to the Committee on Nursing* (London, 1971), paragraphs 62 and 30.

63. Hallam, *Nursing the Image*, p. 182.

64. Hallam, *Nursing the Image*, pp. 183–184.

65. Hallam, *Nursing the Image*, p. 183.

66. A. S. Batata, 'International Nurse Recruitment and NHS Vacancies: A Cross-Sectional Analysis', *Globalization and Health*, 1:7 (2005), 1–10.

67. Report from the Researching Equal Opportunities for Overseas-Trained Nurses and other Healthcare Professionals (ROEH) Study, p. 13.

68. In 2008, initial admissions to the register from overseas numbered 2,309, compared with 14,122 in 2004. The number of initial admissions from England fell from 17,538 to 15,862 in the same period; figures taken from the Nursing and Midwifery Council at http://www.nmc-uk.org.

69. J. Buchan, 'New Opportunities: United Kingdom Recruitment of Filipino Nurses', in J. Connell (ed.) *The International Migration of Health Workers* (New York, 2008), p. 52.

70. Esmail, 'Asian Doctors', p. 830.

71. Decker, 'Overseas Doctors', p. 29.

72. D. Wright, N. Flis and M. Gupta, 'The 'Brain Drain' of Physicians: Historical Antecedents to an Ethical Debate c.1960–76', *Philosophy, Ethics, and Humanities in Medicine*, 3:24 (2008).

73. S. Mullally and D. Wright, 'La Grande Seduction? The Immigration of Foreign-Trained Physicians to Canada, c.1954–76', *Journal of Canadian Studies* (Fall 2007), 67–89.

74. K. Decker, 'Overseas Doctors', p. 31.

75. For the House of Lords judgement follow the links on the BAPIO website at http://www.bapio.co.uk/.

CHAPTER 3: MULTI-CULTURAL MANCHESTER

1. B. Williams, *The Making of Manchester Jewry, 1740–1875* (Manchester, 1976); S. Coates, 'Manchester's German Gentlemen: Immigrant Institutions in a Provincial City 1840–1920', *Manchester Region History Review*, 5:2 (1991–1992), 21–30.

2. P. de Felice, 'Reconstructing Manchester's Little Italy', *Manchester Region History Review*, 12 (1998), 54–65.

3. F. Neal, 'Manchester Origins of the English Orange Order', *Manchester Region History Review*, 4:2 (1990–1991), 12–24.

4. A. Kidd, *Manchester* (Edinburgh, 2002), p. 121.

5. Kidd, *Manchester*, p. 122.

6. S. Hayton, 'The Archetypal Irish Cellar Dweller', *Manchester Region History Review*, 12 (1998), 66–77.

7. Moving Here website, http://www.movinghere.org.Britain/galleries/ histories/jewish/settling/manchester_jewry_1.htm (accessed 16 September 2009).

8. Kidd, *Manchester*, p. 122.

9. Kidd, *Manchester*, p. 122.

10. Kidd, *Manchester*, p. 122.

11. de Felice, 'Reconstructing Manchester's Little Italy', p. 55.

12. H. Adi and M. Sherwood, *The 1945 Manchester Pan-African Congress Revisited* (London, 1995), p. 12.

13. J. Stanley, 'Mangoes to Moss Side: Caribbean Migration to Manchester in the 1950s and 1960s', *Manchester Region History Review*, 16 (2002–2003), p. 41.

14. K. Fitzgerald, *Speaking for Ourselves: Sikh Oral History* (Manchester, no date); P. Werbner, 'Renewing an Industrial Past: British Pakistani Entrepreneurship in Manchester', in J. M. Brown and R. Foot, *Migration: The Asian Experience* (Basingstoke, 1994), pp. 110–112.

15. Stanley, 'Mangoes to Moss Side', p. 41.

16. Stanley, 'Mangoes to Moss Side', p. 41.

17. Stanley, 'Mangoes to Moss Side', p. 43.

18. Manchester Planning Department, *Ethnic Minority Groups in Manchester* (Manchester, 1981), ch. 2, table 2.

19. Stanley, 'Mangoes to Moss Side, p. 43.

20. J. Reid, 'Employment of Negroes in Manchester', *Sociological Review* (NS), 4 (1956), pp. 210–211.

21. P. Werbner, 'Pakistani Migration and Diaspora Religious Politics in a Golden Age', in M. Ember, C. R. Ember and I. Skoggard (eds), *Encyclopedia of Diasporas: Immigrant and Refugee Cultures Around the World* (New York, 2005), p. 476. Manchester Planning Department, *Ethnic Minority Groups*, ch. 2, table 3.

22. Werbner, 'Pakistani Migration', p. 479.

23. P. Werbner, *The Migration Process: Capital, Gifts and Offering among British Pakistanis* (New York, 2002), pp. 50–56.

24. Stanley, 'Mangoes to Moss Side', p. 43; Manchester Planning Department, *Ethnic Minority Groups*, ch. 2.

25. Kidd, *Manchester*, p. 225.

26. Kidd, *Manchester*, p. 215.

27. Kidd, *Manchester*, p. 225.

28. Manchester Planning Studies Group, Manchester City Council, *Manchester Census 1991: Ethnic Groups in Manchester* (Manchester, 1994).

29. Fryer, *Staying Power*, p. 209.

30. Hayton, 'The Archetypal Irish Cellar Dweller', p. 66.

31. de Felice, 'Reconstructing Manchester's Little Italy', p. 60.

32. Williams, *Manchester Jewry*, pp. 9–10, 31, 71, and 335; S. Gewirtz, 'Anti-Fascist Activity in Manchester's Jewish Community in the 1930s', *Manchester Region History Review*, 4:1 (1990), 17–27.

33. Adi and Sherwood, *Pan-African Congress Revisited*, p. 155.

34. Adi and Sherwood, *Pan-African Congress Revisited*, p. 142.

35. Adi and Sherwood, *Pan-African Congress Revisited*, p. 155.

36. G. Padmore (ed.), *Colonial and ... Coloured Unity: A Programme of Action. History of the Pan-African Congress* (London, 1963; original 1947); reprinted in Adi and Sherwood, *Pan-African Congress Revisited*.

37. Padmore, *Colonial*, p. 77.

38. Stanley, 'Mangoes to Moss Side', p. 44.

39. Stanley, 'Mangoes to Moss Side', p. 44.

40. R. Ramdin, *The Making of the Black Working Class in Britain* (Aldershot, 1987), p. 439.

41. Reid, 'Employment of Negroes', 199–211.

42. See J. Ould, *"Strangers in our Midst": Reporting on Immigrant Experiences in the Manchester Evening Chronicle* (Manchester, 2004).

43. W. H. Crawford, 'A Cosmopolitan City', in N. J. Frangopulo (ed.), *Rich Inheritance: A Guide to the History of Manchester* (Manchester, 1962), p. 121.

44. R. Ramdin, *Reimaging Britain: 500 Years of Black and Asian History* (London, 1999), p. 274; Ramdin, *The Making of the Black Working Class*, p. 438.

45. Ramdin, *The Making of the Black Working Class*, p. 439.

46. Manchester City Archives, M184, Manchester Pakistani Welfare and Information Centre Ltd. minutes and correspondence 1967–1968, draft of letter to Town Clerk (G C Ogden) from Dean of Manchester, Chairman, no date.

47. Manchester City Archives, M184, Manchester Pakistani Welfare and Information Centre Ltd. minutes and correspondence 1967–1968, Annual Report 1965–1966, p. 1.

48. S. Chatterjee, *All My Yesterdays* (Stanhope, 2006), pp. 93–95.

49. Chatterjee, *All My Yesterdays*, p. 97.

50. Manchester City Archives, M184, International Council of Manchester and District minutes 1962–1966, accounts 1963–1966 and correspondence 1962–1966, notes on local committees, May 1965.

51. Chatterjee, *All My Yesterdays*, p. 97.

52. D. Renton, 'Anti-fascism in the North West 1976–1981', available at http://www.dkrenton.co.Britain/anl/northw.htm (accessed 19 September 2009).

53. 'Fresh Looting Co-ordinated', *The Guardian*, 9 July 1981, p. 1; '1,000 on Rampage in Moss Side', *The Guardian*, 9 July 1981, p. 1;

54. Sir L. G. Scarman, *The Scarman Report: The Brixton Disorders 10–12 April 1981: Report of an Inquiry* (Harmondsworth, 1982).

55. E. L. Jones and J. V. Pickstone, *The Quest for Public Health in Manchester the Industrial City, the NHS and the Recent History* (Manchester, 2008), pp. 79–80.

56. 'Dr Charan Das Bhagabat', in Ahmed Iqbal Ullah Education Trust, *Roots and Journeys* (Manchester, 2008), pp. 2–9.

57. 'Hospital Nursing Staffs', *The Manchester Guardian*, 9 September 1918, p. 8.

58. 'Hospital Waiting Lists', *The Manchester Guardian*, 3 May 1945, p. 2.

59. See, for example, 'Hospital Beds Out of Use; Shortage of Nurses', *The Manchester Guardian*, 28 April 1954, p. 12.

60. 'Hospital Closes Two Wards; Shortage of Nurses', *The Manchester Guardian*, 11 May 1954, p. 12.

61. 'Mental Hospitals', *The Manchester Guardian*, 25 November 1943, p. 2; 'Nursing Shortage May Close Sanatorium', *The Manchester Guardian*, 8 February 1947, p. 6; 'More Deaths from Paralysis; A Call for Nurses', *The Manchester Guardian*, 26 August 1947, p. 6; 'Nursing Shortage; Ten Months' Wait for Hospital Treatment', *The Manchester Guardian*, 28 October 1950, p. 4; 'Shortage of Nurses; Tuberculosis Hospital is Worst Hit', *The Manchester Guardian*, 11 January 1952, p. 5.

62. The National Archives, MH55/945

63. G. Edwards, *The Road to Barlow Moor: The Story of Withington Hospital, Manchester* (Manchester: 1975), p. 38; 'Manchester and Refugees; Refugee Nurses; Hospital Employment Scheme', *The Manchester Guardian*, 23 November 1938, p. 13.

64. 'Conditions in a Manchester Hospital; Latvian Girl's Allegations Refuted', *The Manchester Guardian*, 15 July 1948, p. 3.

65. The National Archives, MH55/1474.

66. The National Archives, MH55/1474.

67. The National Archives, MH55/1475.

68. Mitchell, 'No claim to be called sick nurses at all', p. 192.

69. Mitchell, 'No claim to be called sick nurses at all', p. 192.

70. 'Accommodation and Recreation; Helping Foreign Students', *The Guardian*, 28 June 1962, p. 17.

71. 'North Fails to Draw Enough Doctors; Shortage of Dentists, Too', *The Guardian*, 11 September 1961, p. 11.

72. B. Pullan and M. Abendstern, *A History of the University of Manchester, 1951–1973, Volume I* (Manchester, 2000), p. 110.

73. 'Expansion of Medical School', *The Guardian*, 7 September 1966, p. 1.

74. 'Junior Doctors Demand Better Hospital Pay', *The Guardian*, 3 December 1965, p. 24.

75. 'Plans to Increase the New St Mary's Rejected', *The Guardian*, 27 April 1960, p. 18.

76. 'North Fails to Draw Enough Doctors; Shortage of Dentists, Too', *The Guardian*, 11 September 1961, p. 11.

77. 'The Cheerful People', *The Daily Mirror*, 5 December 1961, p. 11.

78. 'Plans to Increase the New St Mary's Rejected', *The Guardian*, 27 April 1960, p. 18.

79. 'English Tests Urged for Foreign Doctors', *The Guardian*, 1 April 1972, p. 6.

80. Manchester NHS, *Single Equality Scheme 2008–2011*, p. 5.

81. Manchester NHS, *Single Equality Scheme 2008–2011*, p. 7.

82. Manchester NHS, *Single Equality Scheme 2008–2011*, pp. 5–6.

83. Manchester NHS, *Single Equality Scheme 2008–2011*, p. 5.

84. 'News Analysis: Why Foreign Nurses Hold the Nation's Health in

their Hands', *The Independent Online*, 26 November 2002, available at http://www.independent.co.Britain/life-style/health-and-families/health-news/news-analysis-why-foreign-nurses-hold-the-nations-health-in-their-hands–609349.html (accessed 14 September 2009).

85. 'Pay and Perks Lure Irish Nurses Over the Water to Find a Better Life in NHS', *The Irish Post Online*, 5 May 2004, available at http://archives.tcm.ie/irishpost/2004/05/05/story429.asp (accessed 14 September 2009).

86. 'Passage from India', *The Guardian*, 27 April 2003, p. B2.

87. 'The Spanish Acquisitions', *Health Services Journal*, 112:5834, pp. 28–29.

CHAPTER 4: NURSES, MIDWIVES AND HEALTH VISITORS

1. A. Witz, *Professions and Patriarchy* (London, 1995), p. 165.

2. Baxter, *The Black Nurse*, pp. 18–22.

3. Baxter. *The Black Nurse*, p. 21.

4. Baxter, *The Black Nurse*, p. 9.

5. Interview with Carol Baxter; Baxter, *The Black Nurse*, p. 23.

6. Baxter, *The Black Nurse*, p. 8.

7. Baxter, *The Black Nurse*, p. 21.

8. See Lee-Cunnin, *Daughters of Seacole*.

9. J. Garfield, *Black Angles from the Empire* (London, 2000), chapter 3.

10. T. Clay, *Nurses, Power and Politics* (London, 1987), p. 105.

11. Baxter, *The Black Nurse*, pp. 29–30.

12. L. Ali, 'West Indian Nurses and the NHS in Britain 1950–68', MA thesis, University of York (2000), p. 109.

13. See Baxter, *The Black Nurse*, pp. 25–28.

14. Baxter, *The Black Nurse*, p. 29.

15. Baxter, *The Black Nurse*, p. 32.

16. Edwards, *The Road to Barlow Moor*, p. 35.

17. S. Dhaliwal and S. McKay, *The Work-Life Experiences of Black Nurses in Britain: A Report for the Royal College of Nursing* (London, 2008), p. 28.

18. Baxter, *The Black Nurse*, p. 36; Lee-Cunnin, *Daughters of Seacole*, p. 22.

19. Baxter, *The Black Nurse*, p. 39.

20. L. Da-Cocodia, 'The Probable Effects of Racism in Nursing and Related Disciplines', *International Journal of Social Psychiatry*, 30:17 (1984), p. 20; Baxter, *The Black Nurse*, p. 39.

21. Baxter, *The Black Nurse*, pp. 36–37; Lee-Cunnin, *Daughters of Seacole*, p. 24.

22. See also J. V. Creese, *My Windward Side* (Stockport, 2002), pp. 106–107.

23. Baxter, *The Black Nurse*, p. 57.

24. Baxter, *The Black Nurse*, pp. 42–43; Lee-Cunnin, *Daughters of Seacole*, pp. 22–23; Da-Cocodia, 'The Probable Effects of Racism', p. 20.

25. Baxter, *The Black Nurse*, p. 16.

26. Da-Cocodia, 'The Probable Effects of Racism', p. 19.

27. Da-Cocodia, 'The Probable Effects of Racism', p. 19.

28. Nola Ishmael, 'Why are there so few BME nurses in senior NHS posts?', 6 April 2009, *Nursing Times.net*, available at http://www.nursingtimes.net/forums-blogs-ideas-debate/nursing-blogs/why-are-there-so-few-bme-nurses-in-senior-nhs-posts/5000204.article.

29. Neslyn Watson-Druée, 'Why BME nurses lack opportunities in today's NHS', 20 April 2009, *Nursing Times.net*, available at http://www.nursingtimes.net/why-bme-nurses-lack-opportunities-in-today s-nhs/5000641.article.

30. Interviewee wished to remain anonymous.

31. Interviewee wished to remain anonymous.

32. 'University Attends Manchester Festivals in Bid to Boost Black and Ethnic Minority Admissions' available at http://www.salford.ac.uk/news/details/920 (accessed 26 September 2009).

33. The Quality Assurance Agency for Higher Education, *Subject Review Report: The Manchester Metropolitan University: Nursing* (2000), p. 6.

34. Lee-Cunnin, *Daughters of Seacole*, p. 28.

35. Interviewee wished to remain anonymous.

36. Interviewee wished to remain anonymous.

37. Edwards, *The Road to Barlow Moor*, p. 36.

38. Hallam, *Nursing the Image*, p. 117.

39. M. Miers, *Gender Issues and Nursing Practice* (London, 2000), p. 103.

40. Hallam, *Nursing the Image*, p. 117.

41. Miers, *Gender Issues*, p. 105.

42. Miers, *Gender Issues*, pp. 104–106.

43. S. Halford, M. Savage and A. Witz, *Gender, Careers and Organisations* (Basingstoke, 1997), p. 179.

44. Dhaliwal and McKay, *The Work-Life Experiences of Black Nurses in Britain*.

45. 'Obituary: Louise Da-Cocodia', *Manchester Evening News*.

CHAPTER 5: DOCTORS

1. H. K. Valier and J. V. Pickstone, *Community, Professions and Business: A History of the Central Manchester Teaching Hospitals and the National Health Service* (Manchester, 2008).

2. Community Relations Commission, *Doctors from Overseas: A Case for Consultation* (London, 1976).

3. D. J. Smith, *Overseas Doctors in the National Health Service* (London, 1980); M. Anwar and A. Ali, *Overseas Doctors: Experience and Expectations: A Research Study* (London, 1987).

4. Smith, *Overseas Doctors*, pp. 196–204; Anwar and Ali, *Overseas Doctors*, pp. 77–78.

5. See, for example, A. Esmail, 'Racial Discrimination in Medical Schools', in N. Coker, *Racism in Medicine*, pp. 81–97; P. S. Gill, 'General Practitioners, Ethnic Diversity and Racism', in Coker, *Racism in Medicine*, pp. 99–120.

6. Anwar and Ali, *Overseas Doctors*, p. 29.

7. Esmail, 'Asian Doctors', p. 831.

8. Smith, *Overseas Doctors*, p. 27
9. Smith, *Overseas Doctors*, p. 28.
10. Smith, *Overseas Doctors*, p. 187; Anwar and Ali, *Overseas Doctors*, p. 29.
11. Smith, *Overseas Doctors*, pp. 187–188.
12. Anwar and Ali, *Overseas Doctors*, p. 73.
13. A. Esmail and S. Everington, 'Racial Discrimination against Doctors from Ethnic Minorities', *BMJ*, 306:691–692 (1993).
14. A. Esmail and S. Everington, 'Asian doctors still being discriminated against', *BMJ*, 314:1619 (1997).
15. Anwar and Ali, *Overseas Doctors*, p. 14, table 1.
16. Decker, 'Overseas Doctors', p. 47.
17. Decker, 'Overseas Doctors', p. 33.
18. Gill, 'General Practitioners', p. 106.
19. YingYing Wang, 'Single-Handed General Practice in Urban Areas of Scotland', PhD thesis, University of Glasgow (2008).
20. Wang, 'Single-Handed General Practice'.
21. Decker, 'Overseas Doctors', p. 42.
22. Bornat, Henry and Rahjuram, 'Don't mix race with the specialty', p. 17.
23. Bornat, Henry and Rahjuram, 'Don't mix race with the specialty', pp. 16–17.
24. 'Plans to Increase the New St Mary's Rejected', *The Guardian*, 27 April 1960, p. 18.
25. A. Esmail and P. Abel, 'The Impact of Ethnicity and Diversity on Doctors' Performance and Appraisal', *British Journal of Health Care Management*, 12:10 (2006), 303–307.
26. http://news.bbc.co.uk/1/hi/programmes/newsnight/8163826.stm (accessed on 28 November 2009).
27. Decker, 'Overseas Doctors', p. 47.
28. 'Who Carries the Bedpan?', *The Guardian*, 8 May 1968, p. 5.
29. P. Abel and A. Esmail, 'Performance Pay Remuneration for Consultants in the NHS: Is the Current System Fair or Fit for Purpose?', *Journal of the Royal Society of Medicine*, 99 (2006), 487–493.
30. Abel and Esmail, 'Performance Pay Remuneration', p. 489.
31. British Medical Association, *The Demography of Medical Schools: A Discussion Paper* (London, 2004).
32. British Medical Association, *Equality and Diversity in UK Medical Schools* (London, 2009).
33. British Medical Association, *The Demography of Medical Schools*.
34. *BMJ*, 328(7455): 1518 (26 June 2004).
35. British Medical Association, *The Demography of Medical Schools*, p. 46.
36. L. Cooke, S. Halford and P. Leonard, *Racism in Medical Schools: The Experience of UK Graduates* (BMA, June 2003).
37. http://www.bma.org.uk/healthcare_policy/workforce_issues/social-mobility.jsp (accessed on 2 November 2009).
38. Royal Colleges of Physicians, *Women in Hospital Medicine – Career Choices and Opportunities*: A Report of a Working Party of the

Federation of Royal Colleges of Physicians (London, June 2001).

39. Decker, 'Overseas Doctors', p. 38.

CHAPTER 6: LEARNING FROM THE PAST

1. S. Birch, A. Maynard and A. Walker, *Doctor Manpower Planning in the United Kingdom: Problems Arising from Myopia in Policy-Making*, Discussion Paper 18, Centre for Health Economics, University of York (August 1986), available at http://www.york.ac.uk/inst/che/pdf/dp18.pdf (accessed 4 November 2009).

2. *Workforce Planning, Fourth Report of Session 2006–7*, House of Commons Papers, Health Committee (London, 2007), p. 30.

3. *The Looming Crisis in the Health Workforce: How Can OECD Countries Respond?* (OECD, 2008).

4. Over the period, large proportions of ancillary workers have been from BME groups but unfortunately we have not had the time to address the history of this particular group.

5. A. S. Batata, 'International Nurse Recruitment and NHS Vacancies: A Cross-Sectional Analysis', *Globalisation and Health*, 1:7 (2005), p. 1.

6. C. E. Rosenberg, *Our Present Complaint: American Medicine Then and Now* (Baltimore, 2007), p. 151.

7. K. Robinson, 'The Nursing Workforce: Aspects of Inequality', in J. Robinson, A. Gray and R. Elkan (eds), *Policy Issues in Nursing* (Milton Keynes, 1992), pp. 24–37.

8. Halford, Savage and Witz, *Gender, Careers and Organisations*, p. 179.

9. JC, p. 61.

10. http://www.nwmentoring.nhs.uk/background.html (accessed 3 November 2009).

11. Smith, *Overseas Doctors*, p. 28.

12. Esmail, 'Asian Doctors', p. 831.

13. 'Newly Arrived in United Kingdom', http://www.bapio.co.uk/general_resources/newly_arrived_united_kingdom.html (accessed 15 November 2009).

14. M. Simmgen, 'Why German doctors enjoy British medicine', *Clinical Medicine*, 4:1 (2004), 57–59.

Bibliography and resources

General

Adi, Hakim, and M. Sherwood. *The 1945 Manchester Pan-African Congress Revisited* (London: New Beacon Books, 1995).

Ahmed Iqbal Ullah Education Trust. *Roots and Journeys* (Manchester: Ahmed Iqbal Ullah Education Trust, 2008).

Back, Les, and John Solomos, eds. *Theories of Race and Racism: A Reader* (London and New York: Routledge, 2000).

Berridge, Virginia. *Health and Society in Britain Since 1939* (Cambridge: Cambridge University Press, 1999).

Coates, Su. 'Manchester's German Gentlemen: Immigrant Institutions in a Provincial City 1840–1920', *Manchester Region History Review*, 5:2 (1991–1992), 21–30.

Cohen, Robin, and Zig Layton-Henry, eds. *The Politics of Migration* (Cheltenham UK, and Northampton, Mass.: Edward Elgar Publishing Ltd, 1997).

Crawford, W. H. 'A Cosmopolitan City', in N. J. Frangopulo, ed., *Rich Inheritance: A Guide to the History of Manchester* (Manchester: Manchester Education Committee for the Manchester Teachers' History Discussion Group, 1962), pp. 109–123.

Ellis, Amy. 'UK Resident Population by Country of Birth', *Population Trends*, 135 (2009), 20–28.

de Felice, Paul. 'Reconstructing Manchester's Little Italy', *Manchester Region History Review*, 12 (1998), 54–65.

Fitgerald, Kitty, (in association with Daljit and Raj Kaur Singh and the SFHP Management Committee). *Speaking for Ourselves: Sikh Oral History* (Manchester: Manchester Free Press, no date).

Foot, Paul. *The Rise of Enoch Powell* (Harmondsworth: Penguin Books, 1969).

Fryer, Peter. *Staying Power: The History of Black People in Britain* (London: Pluto, 1984).

Gewirtz, Sharon. 'Anti-Fascist Activity in Manchester's Jewish Community in the 1930s', *Manchester Region History Review*, 4:1 (1990), 17–27.

Gilroy, Paul. *'There ain't no black in the Union Jack': The Cultural Politics of Race and Nation* (London: Hutchinson, 1987).

Halford, Susan, Mike Savage and Anne Witz. *Gender, Careers and Organisations* (Basingstoke: Palgrave Macmillan, 1997).

Hansen, Randall. 'History and Its Lessons' in Sarah Spencer, ed., *The Politics of Migration: Managing Opportunity, Conflict and Change* (Oxford: Blackwell Publishing, 2003).

Hansen, Randall. 'The Kenyan Asians, British Politics, and the Commonwealth Immigrants Act, 1968', *The Historical Journal*, 42:3 (1999), 809–834.

Hayton, Sandra. 'The Archetypal Irish Cellar Dweller', *Manchester Region History Review*, 12 (1998), 66–77.

Jones, Emma L., and John V. Pickstone. *The Quest for Public Health in Manchester the Industrial City, the NHS and the Recent History* (Manchester: Manchester NHS, in association with the Centre for the History of Science, Technology and Medicine, University of Manchester; distributed by Carnegie Publishing, 2008).

Kalra, Virinder S. *From Textile Mills to Taxi Ranks: Experiences of Migration, Labour and Social Change* (Aldershot: Ashgate, 2000).

Kay, Diana, and Robert Miles. *Refugees or Migrant Workers? European Volunteer Workers in Britain, 1946–1951* (London: Routledge, 1992).

Kidd, Alan. *Manchester* (Edinburgh: Edinburgh University Press, 2002).

Kynaston, David. *Austerity Britain, 1945–51* (London: Bloomsbury, 2007).

Manchester Planning Department. *Ethnic Minority Groups in Manchester* (Manchester: Manchester Planning Department, 1981).

Manchester Planning Studies Group, Manchester City Council. *Manchester Census 1991: Ethnic Groups in Manchester* (Manchester: Manchester City Council, 1994).

Miles, Robert. 'Racism and Nationalism in the United Kingdom: A View from the Periphery' in Rohit Bahot, ed., *The Racism Problematic: Contemporary Sociological Debates on Race and Ethnicity* (Lewiston: Lampeter, 1996).

Neal, Frank. 'Manchester Origins of the English Orange Order', *Manchester Region History Review*, 4:2 (1990–1991), 12–24.

Ramdin, Ron. *The Making of the Black Working Class in Britain* (Aldershot: Gower Publishing Company Ltd, 1987).

Ramdin, Ron. *Reimaging Britain: 500 Years of Black and Asian History* (London: Pluto Press, 1999).

Reid, Janet. 'Employment of Negroes in Manchester', *Sociological Review* (NS), 4 (1956), 199–211.

Sales, Rosemary. *Understanding Immigration and Refugee Policy: Contradictions and Continuities* (Bristol: Policy, 2007).

Scantlebury, Elizabeth. 'Muslims in Manchester: The Depiction of a Religious Community', *New Community*, 21:3 (1995), 427.

Scarman, Leslie George. *The Scarman Report: The Brixton Disorders 10–12 April 1981: Report of an Inquiry* (Harmondsworth: Penguin, 1982).

Solomos, John. *Race and Racism in Britain* (Basingstoke: Palgrave Macmillan, 2003).

Thompson, Andrew, and Rumana Begum. 'Asian 'Britishness': A Study of First Generation Asian Migrants in Greater Manchester', *Asylum and Migration Working Paper 4* (Institute of Public Policy Research, 2005).

Visram, Rozina. *Asians in Britain: 400 Years of History* (London: Pluto, 2002).

Werbner, Pnina. *The Migration Process: Capital, Gifts and Offering among British Pakistanis* (New York: Berg, 2002).

Werbner, Pnina. 'Pakistani Migration and Diaspora Religious Politics in a Golden Age', in Melvin Ember, Carol R. Ember and Ian Skoggard, eds, *Encyclopedia of Diasporas: Immigrant and Refugee Cultures Around the World* (New York: Springer, 2004), pp. 475–484.

Werbner, Pnina. 'Renewing an Industrial Past: British Pakistani Entrepreneurship in Manchester, in Judith M. Brown and Rosemary Foot, *Migration: The Asian Experience* (Basingstoke: Macmillan, 1994), pp. 104–130.

Williams, Bill. *The Making of Manchester Jewry, 1740–1875* (Manchester: Manchester University Press, 1976).

Medicine and Nursing

Abel, Pete, and Aneez Esmail. 'Performance Pay Remuneration for Consultants in the NHS: Is the Current System Fair or Fit for Purpose?', *Journal of the Royal Society of Medicine*, 99 (2006), 487–493.

Alexis, Obrey. 'Surviving through Adversity: The Experiences of Overseas Black and Minority Ethnic Nurses in the NHS in the South of England', PhD Thesis, University of Surrey (2006).

Ali, Linda. 'West Indian Nurses and the NHS in Britain 1950–68', MA Thesis, University of York (2001).

Anwar, Muhammad, and Ameer Ali. *Overseas Doctors: Experience and Expectations: A Research Study* (Commission for Racial Equality: London, 1987).

Batata, Amber S. 'International Nurse Recruitment and NHS Vacancies: A Cross-Sectional Analysis', *Globalisation and Health*, 1:7 (2005), 1–10.

Baxter, Carol. *The Black Nurse: An Endangered Species* (Cambridge: Training in Health and Race, 1988).

Beishon, Sharon, Satnam Virdee and Ann Haggell. *Nursing in a Multi-Ethnic NHS* (London: Policy Studies Institute, 1995).

Bheenuck, Shekar. 'Lives and Experiences of Overseas Nurses Working in the British National Health Service', PhD Thesis, University of the West of England (2005).

Bornat, Joanna, Leroi Henry and Parvati Rahjuram, '"Don't mix race with the specialty": Interviewing South Asian Overseas-trained Geriatricians', *Oral History*, 37:1 (2009), 74–84.

Chatterton, Claire S. '"The weakest link in the chain of nursing"? Recruitment and Retention in Mental Health Nursing, 1948–1968', PhD Thesis, University of Salford (2007).

Coker, Naaz, ed. *Racism in Medicine: An Agenda for Change* (London: King's Fund Publishing, 2001).

Community Relations Commission. *Doctors from Overseas: A Case for Consultation* (London: Community Relations Commission, 1976).

Connell, John, ed. *The International Migration of Health Workers* (New York: Routledge, 2008).

Cortis, Joseph D., and A. Shupikai Rinomhota. 'The Future of Ethnic Minority Nurses in the NHS', *Journal of Nursing Management*, 4 (1996), 359–366.

Da-Cocodia, Louise. 'The Probable Effects of Racism in Nursing and Related Disciplines', *International Journal of Social Psychiatry*, 30:17 (1984), 17–21.

Dhaliwal, Sukhwant, and Sonia McKay. *The Work-Life Experiences of Black Nurses in the UK: A Report for the Royal College of Nursing* (London: Royal College of Nursing, 2009).

Doyal, Lesley, Geoff Hunt and Jenny Mellor. 'Your Life in their Hands: Migrant Workers in the National Health Service', *Critical Social Policy*, 1 (1981), 54–71.

Edwards, Gerard. *The Road to Barlow Moor: The Story of Withington Hospital, Manchester* (Manchester: Gerard Edwards, 1975).

Esmail, Aneez 'Asian Doctors in the NHS: Service and Betrayal (William Pickles Lecture)', *British Journal of General Practice* (October 2007), 827–834.

Esmail, Aneez, and Sam Everington. 'Racial Discrimination Against Doctors from Ethnic Minorities', *BMJ*, 306 (1993), 691–692.

Esmail, Aneez, and Sam Everington. 'Asian doctors still being discriminated against', *BMJ*, 314 (1997), 1619.

Esmail, Aneez, and Pete Abel. 'The Impact of Ethnicity and Diversity on Doctors' Performance and Appraisal', *British Journal of Health Care Management*, 12:10 (2006), 303–307.

Great Britain, Committee to Consider the Future Numbers of Medical Practitioners and Appropriate Intake of Medical Students. *Report of the Committee to Consider the Future Numbers of Medical Practitioners and Appropriate Intake of Medical Students* (London: HMSO, 1957).

Hallam, Julia. *Nursing the Image: Media, Culture and Professional Identity* (London: Routledge, 2000).

Hinds, Donald. *Journey to an Illusion: The West Indian in Britain* (London: Heinemann, 1996).

Ishmael, Nola 'Why are there so few BME nurses in senior NHS posts?', *Nursing Times.net* (6 April 2009), available at http://www.nursingtimes.net/forums-blogs-ideas-debate/nursing-blogs/why-are-there-so-few-bme-nurses-in-senior-nhs-posts/5000204.article.

Kyriakides, Christopher, and Satnam Virdee. 'Migrant Labour, Racism, and the British National Health Service', *Ethnicity and Health*, 8:4 (2003), 283–305.

Lee-Cunin, Marina. *Daughters of Seacole: A Study of Black Nurses in West Yorkshire* (Batley: West Yorkshire Low Pay Unit, 1989).

Miers, Margaret. *Gender Issues and Nursing Practice* (London: Macmillan, 2000).

Ministry of Health, Department of Health for Scotland, and Ministry of Labour and National Service. *Report of the Working Party on the Recruitment and Training of Nurses* (London: HMSO, 1947).

Mitchell, Duncan. '"No claim to be called sick nurses at all": An Historical Study of Learning Disability Nursing', PhD Thesis, London South Bank University (2000).

Muldowney, Mary. 'New Opportunities for Irish Women? Employment in Britain during the Second World War' *University of Sussex Journal of Contemporary History*, 10 (2006), 1–18.

NHS Institute for Innovation and Improvement. *Access of BME Staff to Senior Positions in the NHS* (Coventry: NHS Institute for Innovation and Improvement, January 2006).

O'Brien, Theresa A. 'A Study of the Assimilation of Overseas Nurses into the NHS Nursing Cadre', PhD Thesis, Lancaster University (2006).

Raghuram, Parvati. 'Interrogating the Language of Integration: The Case of Internationally Recruited Nurses', *Journal of Clinical Nursing*, 16 (2007), 2246–2251.

Robinson, Kate. *The Nursing Workforce: Aspects of Inequality*, in Jane Robinson, Alastair Gray and Ruth Elkan, eds, *Policy Issues in Nursing* (Milton Keynes: Open University Press, 1992), pp. 24–37.

Rosenberg, Charles E. *Our Present Complaint: American Medicine Then and Now*, (Baltimore: John Hopkins University Press, 2007).

Santry, Charlotte. 'HSJ survey shows 'racism alive in NHS', *Health Service Journal Online* (6 November 2008), available at http://www.hsj.co.uk/hsj-survey-shows-racism-alive-in-nhs/1915075.article.

Seale, John. 'Medical Emigration from Great Britain and Ireland', *BMJ*, 1 (1964), 1173–1178.

Simmgen, Marcus. 'Why German Doctors Enjoy British Medicine', *Clinical Medicine*, 4:1 (2004), 57–59.

Smith, David J. *Overseas Doctors in the National Health Service* (London: Policy Studies Institute, 1980).

Smith Pam A., Helen Allan, Leroi W. Henry, John A. Larsen and Maureen M. Mackintosh. 'Valuing and Recognising the Talents of a Diverse Healthcare Workforce', Report from the REOH Study: Researching Equal Opportunities for Overseas-trained Nurses and Other Healthcare Professionals (European Institute of Health and Medical Sciences, University of Surrey, the Open University and the Royal College of Nursing, 2006).

Stewart, John. 'Angels or Aliens? Refugee Nurses in Britain, 1938 to 1942', *Medical History*, 47 (2003), 149–172.

Tate, Colleen Wedderburn. *Leadership in Nursing* (Edinburgh: Churchill, Livingstone, 1999).

The Quality Assurance Agency for Higher Education, *Subject Review Report: The Manchester Metropolitan University: Nursing* (January 2000 Q215/2000).

Valier, Helen K., and John V. Pickstone. *Community, Professions and Business: A History of the Central Manchester Teaching Hospitals and the National Health Service* (Manchester: Central Manchester and Manchester Children's University Hospital NHS Trust, in association with the Centre for the History of Science, Technology and Medicine, University of Manchester, 2008).

Wang, Ying Ying. 'Single-Handed General Practice in Urban Areas of Scotland', Ph.D. thesis, University of Glasgow (2008).

Watson-Druée, Neslyn. 'Why BME nurses lack opportunities in today's NHS', *Nursing Times.net* (20 April 2009), available at http://www.nursingtimes.net/why-bme-nurses-lack-opportunities-in-todays-nhs/5000641.article.

Webster, Charles. *The Health Services Since the War: Government and Health Care. The National Health Service 1958–1979* (London: Stationery Office, 1996), Volume 2.

Webster, Charles. *The National Health Service: A Political History* (Oxford: Oxford University Press, 1998).

Williams, David R. 'The Concept of Race in Health Services Research: 1966 to 1990', *Health Services Research*, 29:3 (1994), 261–274.

Worboys, Michael, and Lara Marks, eds. *Migrants, Minorities and Health: Historical and Contemporary Studies* (London: Routledge, 1997).

Memoirs and Oral History

Chatterjee, Satya. *All My Yesterdays* (Stanhope: The Memoir Club, 2006).

Creese, Jannett. *My Windward Side* (Stockport: Stockport MBC Community Services, 2002).

Garfield, Judith. *Black Angels from the Empire* (Stratford: Eastside Community Heritage, 2000).

Garvey, Louise Zelph. *Nursing Lives of Black Nurses in Nottingham* (Nottingham: Nottinghamshire Living History Archive Millennium Award Scheme, 2002).

Kramer, Ann. *Many Rivers to Cross: The History of the Caribbean Contribution to the NHS* (London: Department of Health, 2006).

Stanley, Jo. 'Mangoes to Moss Side: Caribbean Migration to Manchester in the 1950s and 1960s', *Manchester Region History Review*, 16 (2003), 40–50.

Archival Collections

The National Archives, Kew:
MH55/944–945, Ministry of Health, Public Health Propaganda – Nursing and Hospital Domestics, Nurses Recruitment Campaign.
MH55/1474–1475, Employment of Women from Barbados from the West Indies as Domestics in Hospitals, 1947–1952, and 1952–1955.
MH55/2157, Migration to and from Britain, 1950–1958.
MH55/2098, Recruitment campaign.

Manchester Local Studies and Archives, Manchester Central Library:

M784, Papers of Bernard Sydney Langton C.B.E. (1914–1982), Race Relations Board Member, Labour Manchester City Councillor and Lord Mayor of Manchester.

M184, International Council of Manchester and District. Minutes, accounts and correspondence, 1962–1966.

M184, Manchester Pakistani Welfare and Information Centre Ltd. Minutes and correspondence, 1967–1968.

Museums

Manchester Jewish Museum: 190 Cheetham Hill Road, Manchester M8 8LW. Website: http://www.manchesterjewishmuseum.com/.

Visual Sources

'Raj to Rhondda: How Asian Doctors Saved the NHS', broadcast on BBC Four, 16 October 2007.

Websites and Online Resources

A full list of BME groups and organisations in Manchester can be found at https://a1.manchester.gov.uk/locgrps.nsf/main

Ahmed Iqbal Ullah Education Trust, Race Relations Resource Centre: http://www.racearchive.org.uk/

Black and Asian Studies Association: http://www.blackandasianstudies.org.uk

BAPIO, British Association for Physicians of Indian Origin: http://www.bapio.co.uk/

BIDA, British International Doctors Association: http://www.bidaonline.org.uk/

Central Manchester University Hospitals NHS Foundation Trust Equality and Diversity pages: http://www.cmft.nhs.uk/trust/equality-and-diversity.aspx

Chronicle World – Changing Black Britain (see especially Archive 03, 02/01/02 on 'Can racism in the National Health Service be cured?'): http://www.chronicleworld.org/

Community Health Involvement & Empowerment Forum (CHIEF): http://www.chiefcic.com/

Eastside Community Heritage – Hidden Histories: http://www.hidden-histories.org.uk/

Manchester City Council, Multi-Cultural Manchester: http://www.manchester.gov.uk/info/448/archives_and_local_studies/506/multi-cultural_manchester/1

Moving Here. 200 Years of Migration in England: www.movinghere.org.uk

Manchester Mental Health and Social Care NHS Trust Equality and Diversity pages:
http://www.mhsc.nhs.uk/page.aspx?p=135

NHS Breaking Through Programme:
http://www.nhsleadtheway.co.uk/breakingthrough.aspx

NHS Manchester Equality and Diversity pages:
http://www.manchester.nhs.uk/pct/equality_and_diversity/

North West Strategic Health Authority 60th Anniversary of the NHS Exhibition:
http://www.northwest.nhs.uk/whatwedo/equalityanddiversity/the 60th anniversary of the nhs.html

Nurses Voices. An Oral History:
http://www.nursesvoices.org.uk/

Pennine Acute Hospitals NHS Trust Equality and Diversity pages:
http://www.pat.nhs.uk/PublicDefault.aspx?tabindex=1&tabid=683

REOH Study: Researching Equal Opportunities for Overseas-trained Nurses and Other Healthcare Professionals:
http://portal.surrey.ac.uk/reoh

Runneymede Trust
http://www.runnymedetrust.org/

UK Association of International Doctors:
http://www.ukaid.org.uk/

University Hospital of South Manchester Equality and Diversity pages:
http://www.uhsm.nhs.uk/patients/Pages/Equalitydiversity.aspx